Praise for *A Year in Provence*

'Stylish, witty and delightfully readable. The style is high comedy and Mayle is bitingly funny about local rural *mores*. But the jokeyness only partly obscures Mayle's warm enthusiasm for local life and landscape. He writes vividly . . . and throws himself with infectious gusto into Provençal sensuality' THE SUNDAY TIMES

'An engaging diary . . . Peter Mayle's idyllic portrait makes you almost taste the wonderful food and wine, feel the sun and balmy breezes, and take part in the games of boules and goat races' SUNDAY EXPRESS

'His sense of humour, which extends to a willingness to laugh at himself, and his keen eye for the absurd, make a strong contribution to an enjoyable book. The accuracy of the descriptive observation makes it advised reading for anyone planning to move to Provence'
THE TIMES LITERARY SUPPLEMENT

'Anyone with any feel for the land and the people who lead their lives close to it will be enchanted'
YORKSHIRE EVENING POST

Toujours Provence

Named as the Travel Writer of the Year in the 1989 British Book Awards, Peter Mayle now lives in the Lubéron with his wife.

TOUJOURS PROVENCE

Peter Mayle
Illustrated by Kevin Hart

PAN BOOKS
LONDON, SYDNEY AND AUCKLAND

To Jennie, as always, and to the friends and partners in research who have been so generous in so many ways: Michel from Châteauneuf, Michel from Cabrières, Henriette and Faustin, Alain the truffle hunter, Christopher, Catherine and Bernard. Mille mercis.

First published in Great Britain in 1991 by Hamish Hamilton Ltd
This edition published 1992 by Pan Books Ltd
a division of Pan Macmillan Limited
Cavaye Place, London SW10 9PG

9

© Peter Mayle 1991
Illustrations © Kevin Hart 1991

The right of Peter Mayle to be identified as author of
this work has been asserted by him in accordance with
the Copyright, Designs and Patents Act 1988.

ISBN 0 330 31947 7

Printed in England by Clays Ltd, St Ives plc

Contents

Foreword

An eyewitness account of the invasion of Provence by 500,000 British thugs

It was an unusual sight, possibly unique in the long history of Ménerbes. A Rolls-Royce had been seen nosing, in its stately fashion, through the village.

To most people, this would have been worth a second glance only because some of the streets of Ménerbes are narrower than a Rolls-Royce, and therefore provide interesting opportunities for a one-car traffic jam. To others, however, the arrival of the Rolls had great and gloomy significance, to be welcomed with as little enthusiasm as the reappearance of the Black Death, or news that cirrhosis of the liver was contagious. An expatriate resident summed it up for the *Sunday Times* in one despairing sentence. 'It is', he said, 'the end of the Lubéron.'

Worse, much worse, was to come, according to another expatriate, a distinguished lady resident of Aix. She claimed that busloads of British hooligans were about to descend on Provence. This was immediately transformed into a precise and infinitely menacing statistic: overnight, through the magic of journalism, mere busloads became 500,000 thugs, probably awash with lager and looking for some vicious diversion to keep them amused until the start of the football season. It was possible, so the distinguished lady from Aix said, that all British expatriates – even those of impeccable rectitude – would be expelled from France, presumably as a punishment for the unspecified but certainly ghastly acts that the thugs would commit. This was reported, with distant relish, in the *New York Times*.

Meanwhile, a part-time Provençal squire muttered about 'Gadarene swine' and the ruination of the spirit of the region, and there were numerous stories (mostly written by experts from their vantage points in Wapping and the Home Counties) of how the peaceful tenor of life in the Lubéron was being destroyed by maddened hordes of tourists.

Throughout the early part of summer, these alarming and curiously repetitive despatches continued to appear. And there I was on the spot, in the seething vortex itself, perfectly placed to observe the horrors of invasion without even having to leave the Café du Progrès.

I spent one morning there in a state of trepidation, half-expecting to witness dreadful scenes of vandalism, mugging, attempted rape, mass intoxication and bellowed demands for fish and chips from an advance party of thugs. As it happened, the dramatic highlight of the morning was a Dutchman falling off his bicycle trying to avoid a cat.

I went further afield, to Goult and Buoux and Cabrières and Bonnieux. Friends there, some of them chefs with a professional interest in tourism, were unable to give me any first-hand reports of the invasion. Tourism was slightly down this year, they felt, undoubtedly because of the recession.

Where were the thugs? Every morning I looked up and down the road outside the house, and every morning it was deserted except for an occasional tractor and the van parked by the side of the melon field. Not a busload of hooligans to be seen. Maybe they'd lost their way, or become trapped on the *périphérique* outside Paris, doomed to go round in circles until they ran out of lager.

By August, I had given up; but other, more diligent reporters were still trying. A camera crew from CBS television arrived at the house one day, hot and puzzled. They had been sent over to film the tourist explosion, and had just spent a couple of hours in Ménerbes.

'Is it always like that?', one of them asked.

'Like what?'

'Kind of empty.'

They had a beer and left to cover a reported outbreak of illegal nude sunbathing in Saint-Tropez.

Ménerbes, 1991

1

Buying Truffles from Monsieur X

The whole furtive business began with a phone call from London. It was my friend Frank, who had once been described in a glossy magazine as a reclusive magnate. I knew him better as a gourmet of championship standard, a man who takes dinner as seriously as other men take politics. Frank in the kitchen is like a hound on the scent, sniffing, peering into bubbling saucepans, quivering with expectation. The smell of a rich *cassoulet* puts him in a trance. My wife says that he is one of the most rewarding eaters she has ever cooked for.

There was a hint of alarm in his voice when he explained why he was calling.

'It's March,' he said, 'and I'm worried about the truffles. Are there still some left?'

March is the end of the truffle season, and in the markets around us, as close as we were to the truffle country in the foothills of Mont Ventoux, the dealers seemed to have disappeared. I told Frank that he might have left it too late.

There was a horrified silence while he considered the gastronomic deprivation that stared him in the face – no truffle omelettes, no truffles *en croûte*, no truffle-studded roast pork. The telephone line was heavy with disappointment.

'There's one man,' I said, 'who might have a few. I could try him.'

Frank purred. 'Excellent, excellent. Just a couple of kilos. I'm going to put them in egg-boxes and keep them in the deep-freeze. Truffles in the spring, truffles in the summer. Just a couple of kilos.'

Two kilos of fresh truffles, at current Paris prices, would have cost more than £1,000. Even down in Provence, by-passing the chain of middlemen and buying direct from the hunters with their muddy boots and leather hands, the investment would be impressive. I asked Frank if he was sure he wanted as much as two kilos.

'It wouldn't do to run short,' he said. 'Anyway, see what you can manage.'

My only contact with the truffle business consisted of a telephone number scribbled on the back of a bill by the chef of one of our local restaurants. He had told us that this was *un homme sérieux* as far as truffles were concerned, a man of irreproachable honesty, which is not always the case in the murky world of truffle dealing where petty swindles are rumoured to be as common as sunny days in Aix. I had heard tales of truffles loaded with buckshot and caked with mud to increase their weight and, even worse, inferior speci-mens smuggled in from Italy and sold as native French truffles. Without a reliable supplier, one could get into some expensive trouble.

I called the number that the chef had given me, and mentioned his name to the man who answered. *Ah, oui.* The credentials were accepted. What could he do for me?

Some truffles? Maybe two kilos?

'*Oh là là*,' said the voice. 'Are you a restaurant?'

No, I said, I was buying on behalf of a friend in England.

'An Englishman? *Mon Dieu.*'

After a few minutes of sucking his teeth and explaining the considerable problems involved in finding so many truffles so late in the season, Monsieur X (his *nom de truffe*) promised to take his dogs into the hills and see what he could find. He would let me know, but it would not be a rapid affair. I must stay by the phone and be patient.

A week passed, nearly two, and then one evening the phone rang.

A voice said, 'I have what you want. We can have a rendezvous tomorrow evening.'

He told me to be waiting by a telephone *cabine* on the Carpentras road at six o'clock. What make and colour was my car? And one important point: cheques were not accepted. Cash, he said, was more agreeable. (This, as I later discovered, is standard practice in the truffle trade. Dealers don't believe in paperwork, don't issue receipts, and regard with disdain the ridiculous notion of income tax.)

I arrived at the phone box just before six. The road was deserted, and I was uncomfortably conscious of the large wad of cash in my pocket. The papers had been full of reports of robberies and other unpleasantness on the back roads of the Vaucluse. Gangs of *voyous*, according to the crime reporter of *Le Provençal*, were out and about, and prudent citizens should stay at home.

What was I doing out here in the dark with a salami-sized roll of 500-franc notes, a sitting and well-stuffed duck? I searched the car for a defensive weapon, but the best I could find was a shopping basket and an old copy of the *Guide Michelin*.

Ten slow minutes went by before I saw a set of headlights. A dented Citroën van wheezed up and stopped on the other side of the phone box. The driver and I looked at each other surreptitiously from the safety of our cars. He was alone. I got out.

I'd been expecting to meet an old peasant with black teeth and canvas boots and a villainous sideways glance, but Monsieur X was young, with cropped black hair and a neat moustache. He looked pleasant. He even grinned as he shook my hand.

'You'd never have found my house in the dark,' he said. 'Follow me.'

We drove off, leaving the main road for a twisting stony track that led deeper and deeper into the hills, Monsieur X driving as if he were on the *autoroute* with me bouncing and clattering behind. Eventually, he turned through a narrow gateway and parked in front of an unlit house surrounded by clumps of scrub oak. As I opened the car door, a large Alsatian appeared from the shadows and inspected my leg thoughtfully. I hoped he'd been fed.

I could smell truffles as soon as I went through the front door – that ripe, faintly rotten smell which can find its way through everything except glass and tin. Even eggs, when stored in a box with a truffle, will taste of truffles.

And there they were on the kitchen table, piled in an old basket, black, knobbly, ugly, delicious and expensive.

'*Voilà*.' Monsieur X held the basket up to my nose. 'I've brushed off the mud. Don't wash them until just before you eat them.'

He went to a cupboard and took out an ancient pair of scales which he hung from a hook in the beam above the table. One by one, testing the truffles with a squeeze of his fingers to make sure they were still firm, he placed them on the blackened weighing dish, talking as he weighed them about his new experiment. He had bought a miniature Vietnamese pig which he hoped to train into a truffle finder *extraordinaire*. Pigs had a keener sense of smell than dogs, he said, but since the normal pig was the size of a small tractor he was not a convenient travelling companion on trips to the truffle grounds below Mont Ventoux.

The needles on the scales hovered and then settled on two kilos, and Monsieur X packed the truffles into two linen bags. He licked his thumb and counted the cash I gave him.

'*C'est bieng.*' He brought out a bottle of *marc* and two glasses, and we drank to the success of his pig-training scheme. Next season, he said, I must come with him one day to see the pig in action. It would be a major advance in detection technique – *le super-cochon*. As I was leaving, he gave me a handful of tiny truffles and his omelette recipe, and wished me *bon voyage* to London.

The scent of the truffles stayed with me in the car on the way home. The following day, my carry-on luggage smelt of truffles, and when the plane landed at Heathrow a heady whiff came out of the overhead locker as I prepared to take my bag past the X-ray eyes of British Customs. Other passengers looked at me curiously and edged away, as if I had terminal halitosis.

It was the time of Edwina Currie's salmonella alert, and I had visions of being cornered by a pack of sniffer dogs and thrown into quarantine for importing exotic substances that might endanger the nation's health. I walked tentatively through Customs. Not a nostril twitched. The taxi-driver, however, was deeply suspicious.

'Blimey,' he said, 'what you got there?'

'Truffles.'

'Oh, right. Truffles. Been dead long, have they?'

He closed the partition between us, and I was spared the usual cab-driver's monologue. When he dropped me at Frank's house, he made a point of getting out and opening the back windows.

The reclusive magnate himself greeted me, and pounced on the truffles. He passed one of the linen bags round among his dinner guests, some of whom were not at all sure what they were sniffing, and then summoned from the kitchen his domestic commander-in-chief, a Scotsman of such statuesque demeanour that I always think of him as a General-Domo.

'I think we need to deal with these at once, Vaughan,' said Frank.

Vaughan raised his eyebrows and sniffed delicately. He knew what they were.

'Ah,' he said, 'the bonny truffle. This will do very well with the *foie gras* tomorrow.'

Monsieur X would have approved.

It was strange to be in London again after an absence of nearly two years. I felt out of place and foreign, and I was surprised how much I had changed. Or maybe it was London. There was endless talk about money, property prices, the stock market and corporate acrobatics of one sort or another. The weather, once a traditional English complaint, was never mentioned, which was just as well. That at least hadn't changed, and the days passed in a blur of grey drizzle, with people on the streets hunched up against the continuous dripping from above. Traffic barely moved, but most drivers didn't seem to notice; they were busy talking, presumably about money and property prices, on their car phones. I missed the light and the space and the huge open skies of Provence, and I realized that I would never willingly come back to live in a city again.

On the way out to the airport, the cab driver asked where I was going, and when I told him, he nodded knowingly.

'I was down there once,' he said. 'Fréjus, it was, in the caravan. Bloody expensive.'

He charged me £25 for the ride, wished me a happy holiday and warned me about the drinking water that had been his downfall in Fréjus. Three days on the khazi, he said. The wife had been well pleased.

I flew out of winter and into spring, and went through the informalities of arriving in Marignane, which I never understand. Marseille is reputed to be the centre of half the drug business in Europe, and yet passengers carrying hand baggage stuffed with hashish, cocaine, heroin, English Cheddar or any other form of contraband can walk out of the airport without going through Customs. It was, like the weather, a complete contrast to Heathrow.

Monsieur X was pleased to hear how welcome his two kilos had been.

'He is an *amateur*, your friend?'

Yes he is, I said, but some of his friends were not too sure about the smell.

I could almost hear him shrug over the phone. It is a little special. Not everyone likes it. *Tant mieux* for those who do. He laughed, and his voice became confidential.

'I have something to show you,' he said. 'A film I made. We could drink some *marc* and watch it if you like.'

When I finally found his house, the Alsatian greeted me like a long-lost bone, and Monsieur X called him off, hissing at him in the way that I had heard hunters use in the forest.

'He's just playful,' he said. I'd heard that before too.

I followed him indoors to the cool, truffle-scented kitchen, and he poured *marc* into two thick tumblers. I must call him Alain, he said, pronouncing it with a good Provençal twang: *Alang*. We went into the sitting-room, where the shutters had been closed against the sunlight, and he squatted in front of the television set to put a cassette into the video machine.

'*Voilà*,' said Alain. 'It is not Truffaut, but I have a friend with a camera. Now I want to make another one, but more *professionnel*.'

The theme music from *Jean de Florette* started, and an image came up on the screen: Alain, seen from the back, and two dogs walking up a rocky hill, Mont Ventoux and its white crest in the far background. A title appeared – *Rabasses de Ma Colline* – and Alain explained that *rabasses* was the Provençal word for truffles.

Despite the slightly shaky hand of the camera operator and a certain abruptness in the editing, it was fascinating. It showed the dogs scenting tentatively, then scrabbling, then digging hard until Alain nudged them aside and, with enormous care, felt under the loosened soil. Every time he came up with a truffle, the dogs were rewarded with a biscuit or a scrap of sausage and the camera would zoom jerkily in to a close-up of an earth-covered hand holding an earth-covered lump. There was no recorded commentary, but Alain talked over the pictures.

'She works well, the little one,' he said, as the picture showed a small, nondescript dog studying the base of a truffle oak, 'but she's getting old.' She began to dig, and Alain came into the shot. There was a close-up of a muddy nose, and Alain's hands pushing the dog's head away. His fingers probed the earth, picking out stones, scooping patiently until he had made a hole about six inches deep.

The film cut suddenly to show the sharp, alert face of a

ferret, and Alain got up and pushed the fast forward button on the video machine. 'That's just rabbit hunting,' he said, 'but there is something else here which is good, and not often to be seen today. It will soon be history.'

He slowed the film down as the ferret was being put, somewhat unwillingly, into a rucksack. There was another sudden cut, this time to a clump of oak trees. A Citroën 2CV van lurched into the picture and stopped, and a very old man in a cloth cap and shapeless blue jacket got out, beamed at the camera and went slowly to the back of the van. He opened the door and took out a crude wooden ramp. He looked to the camera and beamed again before reaching into the back of the van. He straightened up, holding the end of a piece of rope, beamed once more and began to tug.

The van shuddered, and then, inch by inch, the dirty pink profile of a pig's head emerged. The old man tugged again, harder, and the monstrous creature swayed unsteadily down the ramp, twitching its ears and blinking. I half expected it to follow its master's example and leer at the camera, but it just stood in the sun, vast, placid, unaffected by stardom.

'Last year,' said Alain, 'that pig found nearly 300 kilos of truffles. *Un bon paquet.*'

I could hardly believe it. I was looking at an animal that earned more last year than most of those executives in London, and all without the benefit of a car phone.

The old man and the pig wandered off into the trees as though they were taking an aimless stroll, two rotund figures dappled by the winter sunshine. The screen went dark as the camera swooped down to a close-up of a pair of boots and across to a patch of earth. A muddy snout the size of a drainpipe poked into the shot, and the pig got down to work, its snout moving rhythmically back and forth, ears flopping over its eyes, a single-minded earth-moving machine.

The pig's head jerked, and the camera drew back to show the old man pulling on the rope. The pig was reluctant to leave what was obviously a highly desirable smell.

'The scent of truffles to a pig,' said Alain, 'is sexual. That is why one sometimes has difficulty persuading him to move.'

The old man was having no luck with the rope. He bent down and put his shoulder against the pig's flank, and the two of them heaved against each other until the pig grudgingly gave way. The old man reached into his pocket and palmed something into the pig's mouth. Surely he wasn't feeding it truffles at 50 francs a bite?

'Acorns,' said Alain. 'Now watch.'

The kneeling figure straightened up from the earth and turned to the camera, one hand outstretched. In it was a truffle slightly bigger than a golf ball, and in the background the old peasant's smiling face, sun glinting on his gold fillings. The truffle went into a stained canvas satchel, and pig and peasant moved on to the next tree. The sequence finished with a shot of the old man holding out both hands, which were piled high with muddy lumps. A good morning's work.

I was looking forward to seeing the pig being loaded back into the van, which I imagined would require cunning, dexterity and many acorns, but instead the film finished with a long shot of Mont Ventoux and some more *Jean de Florette* music.

'You see the problem with the normal pig,' said Alain. I did indeed. 'I am hoping that mine will have the nose without the . . .' He spread his arms wide to indicate bulk.

'Come and see her. She has an English name. She is called Peegy.'

Peegy lived inside a fenced enclosure next to Alain's two dogs. She was scarcely bigger than a fat corgi, black, pot-bellied and shy. We leant on the fence and looked at her. She grunted, turned her back and curled up in the corner. Alain said she was very amiable, and that he would start training her now that the season was finished and he had more time. I asked him how.

'With patience,' he said. 'I have trained the Alsatian to be a *chien truffier*, although it is not his instinct. I think the same is possible with the pig.'

I said that I would love to see it in action, and Alain invited me to come with him in the winter for a day of hunting among the truffle oaks. He was the complete opposite of the suspicious, secretive peasants who were said to control the truffle trade in the Vaucluse; Alain was an enthusiast, happy to share his enthusiasm.

As I was leaving, he gave me a copy of a poster advertising a milestone in truffle history. In the village of Bedoin, at the foot of Mont Ventoux, there was to be an attempt on a world record: the biggest truffle omelette ever made, to be '*enregistrée comme record mondial au Guinness Book*'. The statistics were astonishing – 70,000 eggs, 100 kilos of truffles, 100 litres of oil, eleven kilos of salt and six kilos of pepper were to be tossed, presumably by a team of Provençal giants, in an omelette pan with a diameter of ten metres. The proceeds were to go to charity. It would be a day to remember, said Alain. Even now, negotiations were in progress to purchase a fleet of brand new concrete mixers which would churn the ingredients into the correct consistency, under the supervision of some of the most distinguished chefs in the Vaucluse.

I said that this was not the kind of event that one normally associated with the truffle business. It was too open, too public, not at all like the shady dealings that were rumoured to take place in the back streets and markets.

'Ah, those,' said Alain. 'It is true there are some people who are a little . . .' he made a wriggling motion with his hand '. . . *serpentin*.' He looked at me and grinned. 'Next time, I'll tell you some stories.'

He waved me off, and I drove home wondering if I could persuade Frank to come over from London to witness the attempt on the omelette world record. It was the kind of gastronomic oddity he would enjoy, and of course Vaughan the General-Domo must come too. I could see him, impeccably turned out in his truffling outfit, directing operations as the concrete mixers swallowed the ingredients: 'Another bucket of pepper in there, *mon bonhomme*, if you please.' Maybe we could find a chef's hat for him, in his clan tartan, with matching trews. I came to the conclusion that I shouldn't drink *marc* in the afternoon. It does funny things to the brain.

2

The Singing Toads
of St Pantaléon

Of all the bizarre events organized to celebrate the mass decapitation of the French aristocracy 200 years ago, one of the most bizarre has so far gone unreported. Not even our local paper, which frequently makes front page stories out of incidents as minor as the theft of a van from Coustellet market or an inter-village *boules* contest – not even the newshounds of *Le Provençal* were sufficiently well informed to pick it up. This is a world exclusive.

I first heard about it towards the end of winter. Two men in the café opposite the *boulangerie* at Lumières were discussing a question that had never occurred to me: could toads sing?

The larger of the two men, a stonemason from the look of his powerful, scarred hands and the fine coating of dust that covered his blue *combinaisons*, clearly didn't think so.

'If toads can sing,' he said, 'then I'm the President of France.' He took a deep pull from his glass of red wine. 'Eh, madame,' he bellowed at the woman behind the bar, 'what do you think?'

Madame looked up from sweeping the floor and rested her hands on the broom handle while she gave the matter her attention.

'It is evident that you're not the President of France,' she said. 'But as for toads . . .' she shrugged. 'I know nothing of toads. It's possible. Life is strange. I once had a Siamese cat who always used the *toilette*. I have colour photographs of it.'

The smaller man leaned back in his chair as if a point had just been proved.

'You see? Anything is possible. My brother-in-law told me there is a man in St Pantaléon with many toads. He is training them for the Bicentenaire.'

'*Ah bon?*' said the big man. 'And what will they do? Wave flags? Dance?'

'They will sing.' The smaller man finished his wine and pushed back his chair. 'By the 14th of July, I am assured that they will be able to perform the Marseillaise.'

The two of them left, still arguing, and I tried to imagine how one could teach creatures with a limited vocal range to reproduce the stirring strains which make every patriotic Frenchman tingle with pride at the thought of noble severed heads dropping into baskets. Maybe it could be done. I had only heard untrained frogs croaking around the house in the summer. The larger and perhaps more gifted toad might easily be able to span more octaves and hold the long notes. But how were toads trained, and what kind of man would devote his time to such a challenge? I was fascinated.

Before trying to find the man in St Pantaléon, I decided to get a second opinion. My neighbour Massot would know about toads. He knew, so he frequently told me, everything there was to know about nature, the weather and any living creature that walked or flew or crawled across Provence. He was a little shaky on politics and property prices, but there was nobody to touch him on wildlife.

I walked along the track at the edge of the forest to the

clammy little hollow where Massot's house was huddled into the side of a steep bank. His three dogs hurled themselves towards me until their chains jerked them up on their hind legs. I stayed out of range and whistled. There was the sound of something falling to the floor and a curse – *putain!* – and Massot appeared at the door with dripping orange-coloured hands.

He came up the drive and kicked his dogs into silence, and gave me his elbow to shake. He had been decorating, he said, to make his property even more desirable when he resumed his efforts to sell it in the spring. Did I not think the orange was very gay?

After admiring his artistic judgement, I asked him what he could tell me about toads. He plucked at his moustache, turning half of it orange before remembering the paint on his fingers.

'*Merde.*' He rubbed his moustache with a rag, spreading paint over his already garish complexion, which the wind and cheap wine had seasoned to the colour of a new brick.

He looked pensive, and then shook his head.

'I have never eaten toads,' he said. 'Frogs, yes. But toads, never. Doubtless there is an English recipe. No?'

I decided not to attempt describing toad-in-the-hole. 'I don't want to eat them. I want to know if they can sing.'

Massot peered at me for a moment, trying to make up his mind whether I was serious.

'Dogs can sing,' he said. 'You just kick them in the *couilles* and then . . .' He lifted his head and howled. 'Toads might sing. Who knows? It is all a question of training with animals. My uncle in Forcalquier had a goat that danced whenever it heard an accordion. It was very droll, that goat, although in my opinion not as graceful as a pig I once saw with some gypsies – now *there* was a dancer. *Très délicat*, despite the size.'

I told Massot what I had overheard in the café. Did he, by any chance, know the man who trained toads?

'*Non. Il n'est pas du coin.*' St Pantaléon, although only a few kilometres away, was on the other side of the main N100 road and was therefore regarded as foreign territory.

Massot was starting to tell me an improbable story about a tame lizard when he remembered his painting, proffered his elbow once again, and went back to his orange walls. On the way home, I came to the conclusion that it was no use asking any of our other neighbours about events taking place so far away. I would have to go to St Pantaléon and continue my researches there.

St Pantaléon is not large, even by village standards. There might be 100 inhabitants, there is an *auberge*, and there is a tiny twelfth-century church with a graveyard cut out of rock. The graves have been empty for years, but the shapes remain, some of them baby-sized. It was eerie and cold that day, with the Mistral rattling the branches of trees, bare as bones.

An old woman was sweeping her doorstep with the wind at her back helping the dust and empty Gauloise packets on their way to her neighbour's doorstep. I asked her if she could direct me to the house of the gentleman with the singing toads. She rolled her eyes and disappeared into the house, slamming the door behind her. As I walked on, I could see the curtain twitch at her window. At lunchtime, she would tell her husband about a mad foreigner roaming the streets.

Just before the bend in the road that leads to Monsieur Aude's workshop – *the Ferronnerie d'Art* – a man was crouched over his Mobylette, poking it with a screwdriver. I asked him.

'*Beh oui*,' he said. 'It is Monsieur Salques. They say he is an *amateur* of toads, but I have never met him. He lives outside the village.'

I followed his directions until I came to a small stone house set back from the road. The gravel on the drive looked as though it had been combed, the mailbox was freshly painted and a business card, protected by perspex, announced in copperplate script, Honoré Salques, *Études Diverses*. That seemed to cover almost any field of study. I wondered what else he did in between supervising choir practice with his toads.

He opened the door as I was walking up the drive and watched me, his head thrust forward and his eyes bright behind gold-rimmed glasses. He radiated neatness, from his precisely parted black hair down to his noticeably clean, small shoes. His trousers had sharp creases and he wore a tie. I could hear the sound of flute music coming from inside the house.

'At last,' he said. 'The telephone has been *en panne* for three days. It is a disgrace.' He pecked his head towards me. 'Where are your tools?'

I explained that I hadn't come to repair his phone, but to learn about his interesting work with toads. He preened, smoothing his already smooth tie with a neat white hand.

'You're English. I can tell. How pleasing to hear that news of my little celebration has reached England.'

I didn't like to tell him that it had been the cause of considerable disbelief as close as Lumières, and since he was now in a good humour I asked if I could perhaps visit the choir.

He made little clucking noises, and wagged a finger under my nose. 'It is clear you know nothing about toads. They do not become active until spring. But if you wish, I will show you where they are. Wait there.'

He went into the house, and reappeared wearing a thick cardigan against the chill, carrying a torch and a large old key labelled, in copperplate script, *Studio*. I followed him through the garden until we came to a beehive-shaped building made from dry, flat stones – one of the *bories* that were typical of Vaucluse architecture 1,000 years ago.

Salques opened the door and shone the torch into the *borie*. Against the walls were banks of sandy soil, sloping down to an inflatable plastic paddling pool in the middle. Hanging from the ceiling above the pool was a microphone, but there was no sign of any of the *artistes*.

'They are asleep in the sand,' said Salques, gesturing with his torch. 'Here' – he shone the torch along the bank at the foot of the left wall – 'I have the species *Bufo viridis*. The sound it makes resembles a canary.' He puckered up his mouth and trilled for me. 'And over here' – the torch swept across to the opposite bank of soil – 'the *Bufo calamita*. It has a vocal sac capable of enormous expansion, and the call is *très, très fort*.' He sank his chin into his chest and croaked. 'You see? There is a great contrast between the two sounds.'

Monsieur Salques then explained how he was going to produce music from what seemed to me to be unpromising material. In the spring, when a *bufo's* fancy lightly turns to thoughts of mating, the inhabitants of the sandy banks were going to emerge and frolic in the paddling pool, singing their songs of love. For reasons of genetic modesty, this would only take place at night, but – *pas de problème* – every birdlike squeak and manly croak would be passed via the microphone to a tape recorder in Monsieur Salques' study. From there, it would be edited, re-mixed, levelled, synthesized and generally transformed through the magic of electronics until it became recognizable as the Marseillaise.

And that was only the beginning. With 1992 soon to be upon us, Monsieur Salques was composing a completely original opus – a national anthem for the countries of the Common Market. Did I not find that an exciting concept?

Far from being excited, my reaction was deep disappointment. I had been hoping for live performances, massed bands of toads with their enormous vocal sacs swelling in unison, Salques conducting from his podium, the star contralto toad delivering a poignant solo, the audience hanging on to every squeak and gribbet. That would have been a musical experience to treasure.

But electronically processed croaking? It was eccentric, certainly, but it lacked the fine untrammelled lunacy of the living toad choir. As for a Common Market anthem, I had serious doubts. If the bureaucrats in Brussels could take years to reach agreement on simple matters like the colour of a passport and the acceptable bacteria count in yogurt, what hope was there of consensus on a tune, let alone a tune sung by toads? What would Mrs Thatcher say?

In fact, I knew what Mrs Thatcher would say – 'They must be *British* toads' – but I didn't want to mingle politics with art, and so I just asked the obvious question.

Why use toads?

Monsieur Salques looked at me as though I was being deliberately obtuse. 'Because,' he said, 'it has never been done.'

Of course.

During the months of spring and early summer, I often

thought of going back to see how Monsieur Salques and his toads were getting on, but I decided to wait until July, when the *concerto bufo* would have been recorded. With luck, I might also hear the anthem of the Common Market.

But when I arrived at the house, there was no Monsieur Salques. A woman with a face like a walnut opened the door, clutching the business end of a vacuum cleaner in her other hand.

Was Monsieur at home? The woman backed into the house and turned off the vacuum cleaner.

Non. He has departed for Paris. After a pause, she added: for the celebrations of the Bicentenaire.

Then he will have taken his music?

That I cannot say. I am the housekeeper.

I didn't want to waste the trip entirely, so I asked if I could see the toads.

Non. They are tired. Monsieur Salques has said they must not be disturbed.

Thank you, Madame.

De rien, Monsieur.

In the days leading up to July 14th, the papers filled with news of the preparations in Paris – the floats, the fireworks, the visiting heads of state, Catherine Deneuve's wardrobe – but nowhere could I find any mention, even in the culture sections, of the singing toads. Bastille Day came and went without a single croak. I knew he should have done it live.

3

Boy

My wife first saw him on the road into Ménerbes. He was walking along beside a man whose neat, clean clothes contrasted sharply with his own disreputable appearance; a filthy rug hung over a framework of bones. And yet, despite the matted coat and burr-encrusted head, it was obvious that this dog was one of a breed peculiar to France, a species of rough-haired pointer known officially as the Griffon Korthals. Beneath that shabby exterior lurked a *chien de race*.

One of our dogs was a Korthals, but they are not often seen in Provence, and so my wife stopped the car to talk to a fellow owner. What a coincidence it was, she said, that she had one of the same unusual breed.

The man looked down at the dog, who had paused to take a dust bath, and stepped backwards to distance himself from the tangle of legs and ears that was squirming in the ditch.

'Madame,' he said, 'he accompanies me, but he is not my dog. We met on the road. I don't know who he belongs to.'

When my wife returned from the village and told me about the dog, I should have seen trouble coming. Dogs are to her what mink coats are to other women; she would like a house full of them. We already had two, and I thought that was quite enough. She agreed, although without conviction, and during the next few days I noticed that she kept looking hopefully down to the road to see if the apparition was still in the neighbourhood.

It would probably have ended there if a friend hadn't called from the village to tell us that a dog just like one of ours was spending every day outside the *épicerie*, drawn by the scent of hams and home-made *pâtés*. Each night he disappeared. Nobody in the village knew his owner. Perhaps he was lost.

My wife had a *crise de chien*. She had found out that lost or abandoned dogs are kept by the Société Protectrice des Animaux (the French RSPCA) for less than a week. If unclaimed, they are put down. How could we let this happen to any dog, let alone a nobly-born creature of undoubted pedigree?

I telephoned the SPA, and drew a blank. My wife began to spend several hours a day in the village on the pretext of buying a loaf of bread, but the dog had vanished. When I said that he had obviously gone back home, my wife looked at me as though I had suggested roasting a baby for dinner. I telephoned the SPA again.

Two weeks passed without sight of the dog. My wife moped, and the man at the SPA became bored with our daily calls. And then our contact at the *épicerie* came up with some hard news: the dog was living in the forest outside the house of one of her customers, who was giving him scraps and letting him sleep on the terrace.

I have rarely seen a woman move so quickly. Within half an hour, my wife was coming back up the drive with a smile visible from fifty yards away. Next to her in the car I could see the enormous shaggy head of her passenger. She got out of the car, still beaming.

'He must be starving,' she said. 'He's eaten his seat belt. Isn't he wonderful?'

The dog was coaxed from his seat and stood there wagging everything. He looked frightful – an unsanitary fur-ball the size of an Alsatian, with a garnish of twigs and leaves entwined in his knotted coat, bones protruding from his body and an immense brown nose poking through the under-growth of his moustache. He lifted his leg against the side of the car and kicked up the gravel with his paws before lying down on his stomach, back legs stretched out behind him and six inches of pink tongue, speckled with fragments of seat belt, lolling from his mouth.

'Isn't he wonderful?' my wife said again.

I held out my hand to him. He got up, took my wrist in his jaws and started to pull me into the courtyard. He had very impressive teeth.

'There you are. He likes you.'

I asked if we could offer him something else to eat, and retrieved my dented wrist. He emptied a large bowl of dog food in three gulps, drank noisily from a bucket of water and wiped his whiskers by hurling himself on the grass. Our two bitches didn't know what to make of him, and neither did I.

'Poor thing,' said my wife. 'We'll have to take him to the vet, and get him clipped.'

There are moments in every marriage when it is futile to argue. I made an appointment with Madame Hélène, *toilettage de chiens*, for that afternoon, since no respectable vet would touch him in his current state. Madame Hélène, I hoped, would be used to the grooming problems of country dogs.

She was very brave about it after her initial shock. Her other client, a miniature apricot-coloured poodle, whimpered and tried to hide in a magazine rack.

'Perhaps it would be best,' she said, 'if I attended to him first. He is very highly perfumed, *n'est-ce pas*? Where has he been?'

'I think in the forest.'

'Mmm.' Madame Hélène wrinkled her nose, and put on a pair of rubber gloves. 'Can you come back in an hour?'

I bought a flea collar, and stopped for a beer in the café at Robion while I tried to come to terms with the prospect of being a three-dog family. There was, of course, always the chance that the previous owner could be found, and then I would have only two dogs and a distraught wife. But in any case, it was not a choice I could make. If there was a canine guardian angel, he would decide. I hoped he was paying attention.

The dog was tethered to a tree in Madame Hélène's garden when I got back, wriggling with pleasure as I came through the gate. He had been clipped down to stubble, making his head look even bigger and his bones even more prominent. The only part of him that had escaped severe pruning was his stumpy tail, which had a whiskery fringe trimmed to a modified pom-pom. He looked mad and extra-ordinary, like a child's drawing of a stick dog, but at least he smelled clean.

He was thrilled to be back in the car, and sat bolt upright on the seat, leaning over from time to time for a tentative nibble at my wrist and making small humming noises that I assumed were signs of contentment.

In fact, they must have been hunger, because he fell on the meal that was waiting for him at home, putting one foot on the empty bowl to keep it still while he tried to lick off the enamel. My wife watched him with the expression most women reserve for well-behaved and intelligent children. I steeled myself, and said that we must start thinking about finding his owner.

The discussion continued over dinner, with the dog asleep under the table on my wife's feet, snoring loudly. We agreed that he should spend the night in an outbuilding, with the door left open so that he could leave if he wanted to. If he was still there in the morning, we would call the only other man we knew in the region who had a Korthals and ask his advice.

My wife was up at dawn, and shortly afterwards I was woken by a hairy face thrust into mine; the dog was still with us. It soon became clear that he was determined to stay, and that he knew exactly how he was going to convince us that life without him would be unthinkable. He was a shameless flatterer. One look from us was enough to set his whole bony body quivering with evident delight, and a pat sent him into ecstasy. Two or three days of this and I knew we would be lost. With mixed feelings, I called Monsieur Grégoire, the man we had met one day in Apt with his Korthals.

He and his wife came over the next day to inspect our lodger. Monsieur Grégoire looked inside his ears to see if he had been tattooed with the number that identifies pedigree dogs in case they should stray. All serious owners, he said, do this. The numbers are stored in a computer in Paris, and if you find a tattooed dog the central office will put you in touch with the owner.

Monsieur Grégoire shook his head. No number. '*Alors*,' he said, 'he has not been *tatoué*, and he has not been fed correctly. I think he is abandoned – probably a Christmas present that grew too big. It happens often. He will be better living with you.' The dog flapped his ears and wagged himself vigorously. He wasn't about to argue.

'*Comme il est beau*,' said Madame Grégoire, and then made a suggestion which might easily have increased the dog population in our house to double figures. What did we think, she asked, about a marriage between the foundling and their young bitch?

I knew what one of us thought, but by then the two women were planning the whole romantic episode.

'You must come up to our house,' said Madame Grégoire, 'and we can drink champagne while the two of them are . . .' she searched for a sufficiently delicate word '. . . outside.'

Fortunately, her husband was made of more practical stuff. 'First,' he said, 'we must see if they are sympathetic. Then, perhaps . . .' He looked at the dog with the appraising eye of a prospective father-in-law. The dog put a meaty paw on his knee. Madame cooed. If ever I had seen a *fait accompli*, this was it.

'But we have forgotten something,' said Madame after another bout of cooing. 'What is his name? Something heroic would be suitable, no? With that head.' She patted the dog's skull, and he rolled his eyes at her. 'Something like Victor, or Achille.'

The dog sprawled on his back with his legs in the air. By no stretch of the imagination could he be described as heroic, but he was conspicuously masculine, and there and then we decided on his name.

'We thought we'd call him Boy. *Ça veut dire garçon en Anglais.*'

'Boy? *Oui, c'est génial,*' said Madame. So Boy he was.

We arranged to take him up to meet his fiancée, as Madame called her, in two or three weeks, after he'd been inoculated, tattooed, fed decently and generally made into as presentable a suitor as possible. In between his trips to the vet and his enormous meals, he spent his time insinuating himself into the household. Every morning he would be waiting outside the courtyard door, squeaking with excitement at the thought of the day ahead, and grabbing the first wrist that came within range. Within a week, he was promoted from a blanket in the outbuilding to a basket in the courtyard. Within ten days, he was sleeping in the house, under the dining table. Our two bitches deferred to him. My wife bought him tennis balls to play with, which he ate. He chased lizards, and discovered the cooling delights of sitting on the steps leading down into the swimming pool. He was in dog heaven.

The day arrived for what Madame Grégoire described as the *rendezvous d'amour*, and we drove up to the spectacular rolling countryside above Saignon where Monsieur Grégoire had converted an old stone stable block into a long, low house overlooking the valley and the village of St Martin-de-Castillon in the far distance.

Boy had gained weight and a thicker coat, but was still lacking in social polish. He bounded from the car and lifted his leg on a newly-planted sapling, churning up a patch of young lawn with his back paws. Madame found him charming. Monsieur, it seemed, was not so sure; I noticed him looking at Boy with a slightly critical eye. Their bitch ignored him, concentrating instead on a series of ambushes mounted against our other two dogs. Boy climbed a hillock at the end of the house and jumped on to the roof. We went inside for tea and cherries marinated in *eau-de-vie*.

'He is looking well, Boy,' said Monsieur Grégoire.

'*Magnifique*,' said Madame.

'*Oui, mais . . .*' There was something worrying Monsieur. He got up and fetched a magazine. It was the latest issue of the official organ of the Club Korthals de France, page after page of photographs showing dogs at the pointing position, dogs with birds in their mouths, dogs swimming, dogs sitting obediently by their masters.

'*Vous voyez*,' said Monsieur, 'all these dogs have the classic coat, the *poil dur*. It is a characteristic of the breed.'

I looked at the pictures. The dogs all had flat, rough coats. I looked at Boy, who was now pressing his great brown nose against the window. His coat had grown after clipping into a mass of grey and brown ringlets which we thought rather distinguished. Not Monsieur Grégoire.

'Unfortunately,' he said, 'he has grown to resemble a *mouton*. From the neck up, he is a Korthals. From the neck down, he is a sheep. I am desolated, but this would be a *mésalliance*.'

My wife almost choked on her cherries. Madame looked dismayed. Monsieur was apologetic. I was relieved. Two dogs and a sheep would do for the time being.

Boy is still, as far as we know, a bachelor.

4

Napoleons at the Bottom of the Garden

At one end of the swimming pool, arranged in a long, low pile, our builders had left an assortment of souvenirs of their work on the house. Rubble and cracked flagstones, old light switches and chewed wiring, beer bottles and broken tiles. It was understood that one day Didier and Claude would come back with an empty truck and take the debris away. The strip of land would be *impeccable*, and we could plant the alley of rose bushes we had planned.

But somehow the truck was never empty, or Claude had broken a toe, or Didier was busy knocking down some distant ruin in the Basses Alpes, and the souvenir pile remained at the end of the pool. In time, it began to look quite pretty, an informal rockery softened by a healthy covering of weeds and splashed with poppies. I told my wife that it had a certain unplanned charm. She wasn't convinced. Roses, she said, were generally considered more attractive than rubble and beer bottles. I started to clear the pile.

In fact, I enjoy manual labour, the rhythm of it and the satisfaction of seeing order emerge from a neglected mess. After a couple of weeks, I reached bare earth and retired in triumph with my blisters. My wife was very pleased. Now, she said, all we need are two deep trenches and fifty kilos of manure, and then we can plant. She got to work with the rose catalogues and I patched up my blisters and bought a pickaxe.

I had loosened about three yards of hard-packed earth when I saw a gleam of dirty yellow among the weed roots. Some long-dead farmer had obviously thrown away a *pastis* bottle one hot afternoon many years ago. But when I cleared away the earth, it wasn't a vintage bottle cap; it was a coin. I rinsed it under the hose, and it shone gold in the sun, the drops of water sliding down a bearded profile.

It was a 20-franc piece, dated 1857. On one side was the head of Napoleon III with his neat goatee and his position in society – *Empereur* – stamped in heroic type opposite his name. On the reverse, a laurel wreath, crowned with more heroic type proclaiming the *Empire Français*. Around the rim of the coin was the comforting statement that every Frenchman knows is true: *Dieu protège la France*.

My wife was as excited as I was. 'There might be more of them,' she said. 'Keep digging.'

Ten minutes later, I found a second coin, another 20-franc piece. This one was dated 1869, and the passing years had left no mark on Napoleon's profile except that he had sprouted a wreath on his head. I stood in the hole that I'd made and did some rough calculations. There were twenty more yards of trench to dig. At the current rate of one gold coin every yard, we could end up with a pocket full of Napoleons and might even be able to afford lunch at the Beaumanière at Les Baux. I swung the pickaxe until my hands were raw, going deeper and deeper into the ground, watching through the beads of sweat for another wink from Napoleon.

I ended the day no richer, but with a hole deep enough to plant a fully grown tree, and the conviction that tomorrow would produce more treasure. Nobody would bury two miserable coins; these had obviously spilled out of the bulging sack that was still lying within pickaxe range, a fortune for the energetic gardener.

To help us estimate the size of the fortune, we consulted the financial section of *Le Provençal*. In a country which traditionally keeps its savings in gold and under the mattress, there was bound to be a listing of current values. And there it was, in between the 1-kilo gold ingot and the Mexican 50-peso piece: Napoleon's 20 francs were now worth 396 francs, and maybe more if the old boy's profile was in mint condition.

Never has a pickaxe been taken up with more enthusiasm, and it inevitably attracted Faustin's attention. He stopped on his way to do battle with the mildew that he was convinced was about to attack the vines, and asked what I was doing. Planting roses, I said.

'*Ah bon?* They must be large roses to need such an important hole. Rose trees, perhaps? From England? It is difficult here for roses. *Tache noire* is everywhere.'

He shook his head, and I could tell he was going to give me the benefit of his pessimism. Faustin is on close terms with every kind of natural disaster, and he is happy to share this extensive knowledge with anyone foolish enough to hope for the best. To cheer him up, I told him about the gold Napoleons.

He squatted at the side of the trench and pushed his cap, stained blue with anti-mildew spray, on to the back of his head so that he could give the news his full attention.

'*Normalement*,' he said, 'where there are one or two

Napoleons, it signifies that there are others. But this is not a good place to hide them.' He waved his large brown paw in the direction of the house. 'The well would be more safe. Or behind a *cheminée*.'

I said that they might have been hidden in a hurry. Faustin shook his head again, and I realized that hurry was not an intellectual concept that he accepted, particularly when it came to hiding sacks of gold. 'A peasant is never as *pressé* as that. Not with the Napoleons. It is just bad luck that they dropped here.'

I said it was good luck for me, and with that depressing thought he went off to look for catastrophe in the vineyard.

The days passed. The blisters flourished. The trench grew longer and deeper. The tally of Napoleons remained at two. And yet it didn't make sense. No peasant would go out to work in the fields with gold coins in his pocket. A *cache* was there somewhere, I was sure of it, within feet of where I was standing.

I decided to seek more advice from the self-appointed expert of the valley, the man from whom Provence held no secrets, the wise, venal and congenitally crafty Massot. If anyone could guess, merely by sniffing the wind and spitting on the ground, where a sly old peasant had hidden his life savings, it was Massot.

I walked through the forest to his house, and heard his dogs baying with frustrated blood lust as they picked up my scent. One day, I knew, they would break their chains and maul every living thing in the valley; I hoped that he would sell his house before they did.

Massot ambled across what he liked to call his front garden, an expanse of bare, trodden earth decorated with dog droppings and clumps of determined weeds. He looked up at me, squinting against the sun and the smoke from his fat yellow cigarette, and grunted.

'*On se promène?*'

No, I said. Today I had come to ask his advice. He grunted again and kicked his dogs into silence. We stood on either side of the rusty chain that separated his property from the forest path, close enough for me to catch his gamey smell of garlic and black tobacco. I told him about the two coins, and he unstuck the cigarette from his lower lip, inspecting the damp stub while his dogs padded back and forth on their chains, growling under their breath.

He found a home for his cigarette under one end of his stained moustache, and leant towards me.

'Who have you told about this?' He looked over my shoulder, as if making sure that we were alone.

'My wife. And Faustin. That's all.'

'Tell nobody else,' he said, tapping the side of his nose with a grimy finger. 'It is possible that there are more coins. This must be kept *entre nous*.'

We walked back along the path so that Massot could see where the two coins had been found, and he gave me his explanation of the national passion for gold. Politicians, he said, were the cause of it, starting with the Revolution. After that, there were emperors, wars, countless presidents – most of them cretins, he said, and spat for emphasis – and devaluations which could turn 100 francs into 100 centimes overnight. No wonder the simple peasant didn't trust scraps of paper printed by those *salauds* in Paris. But gold – Massot held his hands in front of him and wriggled his fingers in an imaginary pile of Napoleons – gold was always good, and in times of trouble it was even better. And the best gold of all was dead man's gold, because dead men don't argue.

How fortunate we are, you and I, said Massot, to come across such an uncomplicated opportunity. It seemed that I had a partner.

We stood in the trench, Massot tugging on his moustache while he looked around him. The ground was flat, some of it planted with lavender, some covered in grass. There was no obvious spot for a hiding place, which Massot took to be an encouraging sign; an obvious place would have been discovered fifty years ago, and 'our' gold removed. He climbed out of the trench, and paced off the distance to the well, then perched on the stone wall.

'It could be anywhere here,' he said, and waved his arm over fifty square yards of ground. '*Évidemment*, that is too much for you to dig.' Our partnership clearly didn't extend to a sharing of physical labour. 'What we need is a *machin* for detecting metal.' He turned his arm into a metal detector and passed it in sweeps over the grass, making clicking sounds. '*Beh oui*. That will find it.'

'*Alors, qu'est-ce qu'on fait?*' Massot made the universal money gesture, rubbing his fingers and thumb together. It was time for a business meeting.

We agreed that I would finish digging the trench, and that Massot would take care of the high technology by renting a metal detector. All that remained to be decided was the financial participation of the partners. I suggested that 10 per cent would be a reasonable price to pay for some undemanding work with a metal detector; Massot, however, said he would be more comfortable with 50 per cent. There was the drive into Cavaillon to pick up the metal detector, the digging involved when we struck gold and, most important, the confidence I could feel in having a completely trustworthy partner who would not broadcast the details of our new wealth throughout the neighbourhood. Everything, said Massot, must be kept behind the teeth.

I looked at him as he smiled and nodded, and thought that it would be difficult to imagine a more untrustworthy old rogue this side of the bars of Marseille prison. Twenty per cent, I said. He winced, sighed, accused me of being a *grippe-sou* and settled for 25 per cent. We shook hands on it, and he spat in the trench for luck as he left.

That was the last I saw of him for several days. I finished the trench, laced it with manure and ordered the roses. The man who delivered them told me that I'd dug far too deep, and asked me why, but I kept the reason behind my teeth.

There is a widespread aversion in Provence to anything that resembles social planning. The Provençal prefers to drop in and surprise you rather than call first to make sure you're free. When he arrives, he expects you to have time for the pleasantries of a drink and a roundabout conversation before getting down to the purpose of the visit, and if you tell him you have to go out he is puzzled. Why rush? Half an hour is nothing. You'll only be late, and that's normal.

It was almost twilight, the time of day *entre chien et loup*, when we heard a van rattle to a stop outside the house. We were going over to see some friends for dinner in Goult, and so I went out to head off the visitor before he reached the bar and became impossible to dislodge.

The van had its back doors wide open, and was rocking from side to side. There was a thud as something hit the floor, followed by a curse. *Putaing!* It was my business partner, wrestling with a pickaxe that was stuck in the metal grill of the dog guard behind the driver's seat. With a final convulsion the pickaxe was wrenched free and Massot emerged backwards, slightly faster than he'd intended.

He was wearing camouflage trousers and a dun sweater and a jungle-green army surplus hat, all well past their youth. He looked like a badly paid mercenary as he unloaded his equipment and laid it on the ground – the pickaxe, a long-handled mason's shovel and an object wrapped in old sacking. Glancing round to see if anyone was watching, he removed the sacking and held up the metal detector.

'*Voilà!* This is *haut de gamme*, top of the range. It is efficacious to a depth of three metres.'

He switched it on, and waved it over his tools. Sure enough, it detected a shovel and a pickaxe, chattering away like a set of agitated false teeth. Massot was delighted. '*Vous voyez?* When he finds metal, he talks. Better than digging, eh?'

I said that it was very impressive, and that I'd keep it safely locked up in the house until tomorrow.

'Tomorrow?' said Massot. 'But we must start now.'

I said it would be dark in half an hour, and Massot nodded patiently, as though I had finally grasped a very complex theory.

'Exactly!' He put down the metal detector and took hold of my arm. 'We don't want the world watching us, do we? This kind of work is best done at night. It is more *discret. Allez!* You bring the tools.'

There is another difficulty, I said. My wife and I are going out.

Massot stopped dead and stared at me, his eyebrows drawing themselves up to their full height in astonishment.

'Out? Tonight? *Now?*'

My wife called from the house. We were already late.

Massot shrugged at the curious hours we kept, but insisted that tonight was the night. He would have to do it all, he said plaintively, himself. Could I lend him a torch? I showed him how to switch on the spotlight behind the well, which he adjusted so that it lit the area by the rose bed, muttering in irritation at being left *tout seul*.

We stopped half-way down the drive and looked back at Massot's elongated shadow moving through the trees, which were bathed in the glow of the spotlight. The ticking of the metal detector carried clearly on the evening air, and I had misgivings about the secrecy of the enterprise. We might as well have put up a sign at the end of the drive saying MAN LOOKING FOR GOLD.

We told our friends over dinner about the treasure hunt which was going on more or less under the cover of darkness. The husband, who had been born and raised in the Lubéron, was not optimistic. He told us that when metal detectors had first become available they were more popular with the peasants than hunting dogs. It was true that some gold had been found. But now, he said, the area had been combed so thoroughly that Massot would be lucky to find an old horse-shoe.

Even so, he couldn't deny the existence of our two Napoleons. There they were, on the table in front of him. He picked them up and chinked them in his hand. Who knows? Maybe we'd be lucky. Or maybe Massot would be lucky and we'd never hear about it. Was he someone who could be trusted? My wife and I looked at each other and decided it was time to go.

It was just after midnight when we got home, and Massot's van had gone. The spotlight had been switched off, but there was enough of a moon for us to see large mounds of earth scattered haphazardly across what we were trying to turn into a lawn. We decided to face the full extent of the damage in the morning.

It was as if a giant mole, maddened by claustrophobia, had been coming up for air and spitting out mouthfuls of metal. There were nails, fragments of a cartwheel rim, an ancient screwdriver, half a sickle, a dungeon-sized key, a brass rifle shell, bolts, bottle tops, the crumbling remains of a hoe, knife blades, the bottom of a sieve, birds' nests of baling wire, unidentifiable blobs of pure rust. But no gold.

Most of the newly planted rose bushes had survived, and the lavender bed was intact. Massot must have run out of enthusiasm.

I left him to sleep until the afternoon before going over to hear his account of the night's work. Long before I reached his house, I could hear the metal detector, and I had to shout twice to get him to look up from the bramble-covered hillock that he was sweeping. He bared his dreadful teeth in welcome. I was surprised to see him so cheerful. Maybe he had found something after all.

'*Salut!*' He shouldered the metal detector like a gun and waded towards me through the undergrowth, still smiling. I said he looked like a man who had been lucky.

Not yet, he said. He had been obliged to stop the previous night because my neighbours had shouted at him, complaining about the noise. I didn't understand. Their house is 250 yards away from where he had been working. What had he been doing to keep them awake?

'*Pas moi,*' he said. '*Lui,*' and he tapped the metal detector. 'Wherever I went, he found something – *tak tak tak tak tak.*'

But no gold, I said.

Massot leaned so close that for one awful moment I thought he was going to kiss me. His nose twitched, and his voice dropped to a wheezing whisper. 'I know where it is.' He drew back and took a deep breath. '*Beh oui.* I know where it is.'

Although we were standing in the forest, with the nearest human being at least a kilometre away, Massot's fear of being overheard was contagious, and I found myself whispering too.

'Where is it?'

'At the end of the *piscine.*'

'Under the roses?'

'Under the *dallage.*'

'Under the *dallage*?'

'*Oui. C'est certaing.* On my grandmother's head.'

This was not the straightforward good news that Massot obviously thought it was. The *dallage* round the pool was made up of flagstones that were nearly three inches thick. They had been laid on a bed of reinforced concrete, as deep as the flagstones were thick. It would be a demolition job just to get down to the earth. Massot sensed what I was thinking, and put the metal detector down so that he could talk with both hands.

'In Cavaillon,' he said, 'you can rent a *marteau-piqueur*. It will go through anything. *Paf!*'

He was quite right. A miniature jack-hammer would go through the flagstones, the reinforced concrete, the pipes feeding the pool and the electric cables leading from the filtration pump in no time at all. *Paf!* And maybe even *Boum!* And when the dust had settled, we might very easily find nothing more than another sickle blade to add to our collection. I said no. With infinite regret, but no.

Massot took the decision well, and was pleased with the bottle of *pastis* I gave him for his trouble. But I see him from time to time standing on the path at the back of the house, looking down at the swimming pool, sucking thoughtfully at his moustache. God knows what he might do one drunken night if someone ever gave him a *marteau-piqueur* for Christmas.

5

Les Invalides

I had been to a pharmacy in Apt for toothpaste and suntan oil, two innocent and perfectly healthy purchases. When I arrived home and took them out of the bag, I found that the girl who served me had included an instructive but puzzling gift. It was an expensively printed leaflet in full colour. On the front was a picture of a snail sitting on the lavatory. He looked doleful, as if he'd been there for some time without achieving anything worthwhile. His horns drooped. His eyes were lack-lustre. Above this sad picture was printed *La Constipation*.

What had I done to deserve this? Did I look constipated? Or was the fact that I bought toothpaste and suntan oil somehow significant to the expert pharmacist's eye – a hint that all was not well in my digestive system? Maybe the girl knew something I didn't know. I started to read the leaflet.

'Nothing,' it said, 'is more banal and more frequent than constipation.' About 20 per cent of the French population, so the writer claimed, suffered from the horrors of *ballonnement* and *gêne abdominale*. And yet, to a casual observer, like myself, there were no obvious signs of discomfort among the people on the streets, in the bars and cafés, or even in the restaurants – where presumably 20 per cent of the clientele tucking into two substantial meals a day were doing so in spite of their *ballonnements*. What fortitude in the face of adversity!

I had always thought of Provence as one of the healthier places in the world. The air is clean, the climate is dry, fresh fruit and vegetables are abundantly available, cooking is done with olive oil, stress doesn't seem to exist – there could hardly be a more wholesome set of circumstances. And everybody looks very well. But if 20 per cent of those ruddy faces and hearty appetites were concealing the suffering caused by a traffic jam in the *transit intestinal*, what else might they be concealing? I decided to pay closer attention to Provençal complaints and remedies, and gradually became aware that there is indeed a local affliction, which I think extends to the entire country. It is hypochondria.

A Frenchman never feels out of sorts; he has a *crise*. The most popular of these is a *crise de foie*, when the liver finally rebels against the punishment inflicted by *pastis*, five-course meals, tots of *marc* and the *vin d'honneur* served at everything from the opening of a car showroom to the annual meeting of the village Communist party. The simple cure is no alcohol and plenty of mineral water, but a much more satisfactory solution – because it supports the idea of illness rather than admitting self-indulgence – is a trip to the pharmacy and a consultation with the sympathetic white-coated lady behind the counter.

I used to wonder why most pharmacies have chairs arranged between the surgical trusses and the *cellulite* treatment kits, and now I know. It is so that one can wait more comfortably while Monsieur Machin explains, in great whispered detail and with considerable massaging of the engorged throat, the tender kidney, the reluctant intestine or whatever else ails him, how he came to this painful state. The pharmacist, who is trained in patience and diagnosis, listens carefully, asks a few questions and then proposes a number of possible solutions. Packets and pots and ampoules are produced. More discussion. A choice is finally made, and Monsieur Machin carefully folds up the vital pieces of paper which will enable him to claim back most of the cost of his medication from Social Security. Fifteen or twenty minutes have passed, and everyone moves up a chair.

These trips to the pharmacy are only for the more robust invalids. For serious illness, or imaginary serious illness, there is, even in relatively remote country areas like ours, a network of first aid specialists which amazes visitors from cities where you need to be a millionaire before you can be sick in comfort. All the towns, and many of the villages, have their own ambulance services, on call twenty-four hours a day. Registered nurses will come to the house. *Doctors* will come to the house, a practice which I'm told is almost extinct in London.

We had a brief but intense experience of the French medical system early last summer. The guinea pig was Benson, a young American visitor on his first trip to Europe. When I picked him up at Avignon station, he croaked hello, coughed, and clapped a handkerchief to his mouth. I asked him what was the matter.

He pointed to his throat, and made wheezing noises.

'Mono,' he said.

Mono? I had no idea what that was, but I did know that Americans have much more sophisticated ailments than we do – haematomas instead of bruises, migraine instead of a headache, post-nasal drip – and so I muttered something about fresh air soon clearing it up and helped him into the car. On the way home, I learned that mono was the intimate form of address for mononucleosis, a viral infection. One symptom is a painful throat. 'Like broken glass,' said Benson, huddled behind his sunglasses and his handkerchief. 'We have to call my brother in Brooklyn. He's a doctor.'

We got back to the house to find the phone out of order. It was the beginning of a long holiday weekend, and so we would be without it for three days, normally a blessing. But Brooklyn had to be called. There was one particular antibiotic, a *state of the art* antibiotic, that Benson said would overcome all known forms of mono. I went down to the phone box at Les Baumettes and fed it with 5-franc pieces while Brooklyn hospital searched for Benson's brother. He gave me the name of the wonder drug. I called a doctor and asked him if he could come to the house.

He arrived within an hour, and inspected the invalid, who was resting behind his sunglasses in a darkened room.

'*Alors, monsieur . . .*' the doctor began, but Benson cut him short.

'Mono,' he said, pointing at his throat.

'*Comment?*'

'Mono, man. Mononucleosis.'

'*Ah, mononucléose. Peut-être, peut-être.*'

The doctor looked into Benson's angry throat and took a swab. He wanted to run a laboratory test on the virus. And now, would Monsieur lower his trousers? He took out a syringe, which Benson peered at suspiciously over his shoulder as he slowly dropped his Calvin Klein jeans to half mast.

'Tell him I'm allergic to most antibiotics. He should call my brother in Brooklyn.'

'*Comment?*'

I explained the problem. Did the doctor by any chance have the wonder drug in his bag? *Non.* We looked at each other round Benson's bare buttocks. They jerked as Benson coughed painfully. The doctor said he must be given something to reduce the inflammation, and that side-effects from this particular shot were extremely rare. I passed the news on to Benson.

'Well . . . OK.' He bent over, and the doctor injected with a flourish, like a matador going in over the horns. '*Voilà!*'

While Benson waited for allergic reactions to send him reeling, the doctor told me that he would arrange for a nurse to come twice a day to give further injections, and that the test results would be through on Saturday. As soon as he had them, he would make out the necessary prescriptions. He wished us a *bonne soirée.* Benson communed noisily with his handkerchief. I thought a *bonne soirée* was unlikely.

The nurse came and went, the test results came through and the doctor reappeared on Saturday evening as promised. The young Monsieur had been correct. It was *mononucléose,* but we would conquer it with the resources of French medicine. The doctor began to scribble like a poet on heat. As prescription after prescription flowed from his pen, it seemed as though every single resource was going to be called into action. He passed over a wad of hieroglyphics, and wished us a *bon weekend.* That too was unlikely.

The Sunday of a holiday weekend in rural France is not the easiest time to find a pharmacy which is open for business, and the only one for miles around was the *pharmacie de garde* on the outskirts of Cavaillon. I was there at 8.30, and joined a man clutching a wad of prescriptions almost as thick as mine. Together we read the notice taped to the glass door: opening time was not until 10.00.

The man sighed, and looked me up and down.

'Are you an emergency?'

No. It was for a friend.

He nodded. He himself had an important *arthrose* in his shoulder, and also some malign fungus of the feet. He was not going to stand for an hour and a half in the sun to wait for the pharmacy to open. He sat down on the pavement next to the door and started to read chapter one of his prescriptions. I decided to go and have breakfast.

'Come back well before ten,' he said. 'There will be many people today.'

How did he know? Was a Sunday morning visit to the pharmacy a regular pre-lunch treat? I thanked him and ignored his advice, killing time with an old copy of *Le Provençal* in a café.

When I returned to the pharmacy just before ten, it looked as though *le tout* Cavaillon had gathered outside. There were dozens of them standing with their voluminous prescriptions, swapping symptoms in the manner of an angler describing a prize fish. Monsieur *Angine* boasted about his sore throat. Madame *Varices* countered with the history of her varicose veins. The halt and the maimed chattered away cheerfully, consulting their watches and pressing ever closer to the still-locked door. At last, to a murmured accompaniment of *enfin* and *elle arrive*, a girl appeared from the back of the pharmacy, opened up, and stepped smartly aside as the stampede jostled through. Not for the first time, I realized that the Anglo-Saxon custom of the orderly queue has no place in French life.

I must have been there for half an hour before I was able

to take advantage of a gap in the scrum and give my documents to the pharmacist. She produced a plastic shopping bag and started to fill it with boxes and bottles, rubber-stamping each prescription as she worked her way through the pile, a copy for her, a copy for me. With the bag at bursting point, one prescription remained. After disappearing for five minutes, the pharmacist admitted defeat; she was out of stock of whatever it was, and I would have to get it from another pharmacy. However, it was not grave, because the important medication was all there in the bag. Enough, it seemed to me, to bring a regiment back from the dead.

Benson sucked and gargled and inhaled his way through the menu. By the next morning he had emerged from the shadow of the grave and was feeling sufficiently recovered to join us on a trip to the Ménerbes pharmacy in search of the last prescription.

One of the village elders was there when we arrived, perched on a stool while his shopping bag was being stuffed full of nostrums. Curious about what exotic disease the foreigners might have, he remained seated while our prescription was being filled, leaning forward to see what was in the packet as it was put on the counter.

The pharmacist opened the packet and took out a foil-wrapped object the size of a deformed Alka-Seltzer tablet. She held it up to Benson.

'*Deux fois par jour*,' she said.

Benson shook his head and put his hand to his throat.

'Too big,' he said. 'I couldn't swallow anything that size.'

We translated for the pharmacist, but before she could reply the old man collapsed with laughter, rocking perilously on his stool and wiping his eyes with the back of a knobbly hand.

The pharmacist smiled, and made delicate upward motions with the foil-wrapped lump. '*C'est un suppositoire.*'

Benson looked bewildered. The old man, still laughing, hopped down from the stool and took the suppository from the pharmacist.

'*Regardez,*' he said to Benson. '*On fait comme ça.*'

He moved away from the counter to give himself space, bent forward, holding the suppository above his head and then, with a flowing backwards swoop of his arm, applied the suppository firmly to the seat of his trousers. '*Tok!*' said the old man. He looked up at Benson. '*Vous voyez?*'

'Up the *ass?*' Benson shook his head again. 'Hey, that's weird. Jesus.' He put on his sunglasses and moved a couple of paces backwards. 'We don't do that where I come from.'

We tried to explain that it was a very efficient method of getting medication into the bloodstream, but he wasn't convinced. And when we said that it wouldn't give him a sore throat either, he wasn't amused. I often wonder what he told his brother the doctor back in Brooklyn.

Shortly afterwards, I met Massot in the forest and told him about the suppository lesson. It was droll, he thought, but for a truly *dramatique* episode there was nothing to touch the story of the man who had gone into hospital to have his appendix out and had woken up with his left leg amputated. *Beh oui.*

I said it couldn't be true, but Massot insisted that it was.

'If I am ever ill,' he said, 'I go to the vet. You know where you are with vets. I don't trust doctors.'

Fortunately, Massot's view of the French medical profession is as unlikely to reflect reality as most of his views. There may be doctors with a taste for amputation in Provence, but we have never met them. In fact, apart from our brush with mononucleosis, we've only seen the doctor once, and that was to combat an attack of bureaucracy.

It was the climax of months of paper-shuffling which we had gone through in order to get our *cartes de séjour* – the identity cards that are issued to foreign residents of France. We had been to the *Mairie*, to the *Préfecture*, to the *Bureau des Impôts* and back again to the *Mairie*. Everywhere we went, we were told that another form was required which, *naturellement*, could only be obtained somewhere else. In the end, when we were convinced that we had a full set of certificates, attestations, declarations, photographs and vital statistics, we made what we thought would be our last triumphal visit to the *Mairie*.

Our dossiers were examined carefully. Everything seemed to be in order. We were not going to be a drain on the state. We had no criminal record. We were not seeking to steal employment from French workers. *Bon*. The dossiers were closed. At last we were going to be official.

The secretary of the *Mairie* smiled nicely, and passed over two more forms. It was necessary, she said, to have a medical examination to prove that we were of sound mind and body. Doctor Fenelon in Bonnieux would be pleased to examine us. Off to Bonnieux we went.

Doctor Fenelon was charming and brisk as he X-rayed us and took us through the fine print of a short questionnaire. Were we mad? No. Epileptic? No. Addicted to drugs? Alcoholic? Prone to fainting? I was half expecting to be interrogated about bowel movements in case we might be adding to the constipated sector of the French population, but that didn't seem to be a concern of the immigration authorities. We signed forms. Doctor Fenelon signed the forms. Then he opened a drawer and produced two more forms.

He was apologetic. '*Bien sûr, vous n'avez pas le problème, mais . . .*' He shrugged, and explained that we must take the forms into Cavaillon and have a blood test before he could give us our *certificats sanitaires*.

Was there anything special that we were being tested for?

'*Ah, oui.*' He looked even more apologetic. '*La syphilis.*'

6

The English Écrevisse

'Writing is a dog's life, but the only life worth living.' That was Flaubert's opinion, and it is a fair expression of the way it feels if you choose to spend your working days putting words down on pieces of paper.

For most of the time, it's a solitary, monotonous business. There is the occasional reward of a good sentence – or rather, what you think is a good sentence, since there's nobody else to tell you. There are long, unproductive stretches when you consider taking up some form of regular and useful employment like chartered accountancy. There is constant doubt that anyone will want to read what you're writing, panic at missing deadlines that you have imposed on yourself, and the deflating realization that those deadlines couldn't matter less to the rest of the world. A thousand words a day, or nothing; it makes no difference to anyone else but you. That part of writing is undoubtedly a dog's life.

What makes it worth living is the happy shock of discovering that you have managed to give a few hours of entertainment to people you've never met. And if some of them should write to tell you, the pleasure of receiving their letters is like applause. It makes up for all the grind. You abandon thoughts of a career in accountancy and make tentative plans for another book.

My first letter arrived shortly after the publication in April of *A Year in Provence*. It came from Luxembourg, polite and complimentary, and I kept looking at it all day. The next week a man wrote asking how to grow truffles in New Zealand. Then the letters began to arrive in a steady trickle – from London, from Beijing, from Queensland, from Her Majesty's Prison at Wormwood Scrubs, from the expatriate community on the Côte d'Azur, from the wilds of Wiltshire and the Surrey hills – some on embossed, true blue, toff's writing paper, others on pages torn from exercise books, one on the back of a map of the London Underground. The addresses were often so vague that the Post Office had to perform small marvels of deduction: '*Les Anglais*, Bonnieux' found us, despite the fact that we don't live in Bonnieux. So did my favourite: '*L'Écrevisse Anglais*, Ménerbes, Provence.'

The letters were friendly and encouraging, and whenever there was an address to reply to, I replied, thinking that would be the end of it. But often it wasn't. Before long we found ourselves in the undeserved position of resident advisers on every aspect of Provençal life from buying a house to finding a baby-sitter. A woman telephoned from Memphis to ask about the burglary rate in the Vaucluse. A photographer from Essex wanted to know if he could make a living taking pictures in the Lubéron. Couples thinking about moving to Provence wrote pages of questions. Would their children fit in to the local schools? How high was the cost of living? What about doctors? What about income tax? Was it lonely? Would they be happy? We answered as best we could, but it was slightly uncomfortable to be involved in the personal decisions of total strangers.

And then, as summer set in, what had been dropping through the mailbox started coming up the drive. Letters turned into people.

It was hot and dry, and I was doing some Provençal weeding in the bone-hard ground with a pickaxe when a car arrived and the driver emerged with a broad smile, waving a copy of my book at me.

'Tracked you down!' he said. 'Did a little detective work in the village. No trouble at all.'

I signed the book and felt like a real author, and when my wife came back from Cavaillon she was properly impressed. 'A fan,' she said. 'You should have taken a photograph. How amazing that someone should bother.'

She was less impressed a few days later when we were leaving the house to go out to dinner and found a pretty blonde lurking behind the cypress tree in the front garden.

'Are you him?' asked the blonde.

'Yes,' said my wife. 'What a pity. We're just going out.' Blondes are probably used to reactions like that from wives. She left.

'That might have been a fan,' I said to my wife.

'She can go and be a fan somewhere else,' she said. 'And you can take that smirk off your face.'

During July and August we became used to finding unfamiliar faces at the front door. Most of them were apologetic and well-mannered, just wanting their books signed, grateful for a glass of wine and a few minutes sitting in the courtyard out of the heat of the sun. They all seemed to be fascinated by the stone table we had finally managed to install with such difficulty.

'So *this* is The Table,' they'd say, walking round it and running their fingers over the surface as if it was one of

Henry Moore's best efforts. It was a very curious sensation to have ourselves, our dogs (who loved it) and our house inspected with such interest. And, I suppose inevitably, there were times when it wasn't curious, but irritating, when a visit felt more like an invasion.

Unseen by us one afternoon when the temperature was over 100°, the husband, the wife and the wife's friend, noses and knees sunburned to a matching angry red, had parked at the end of the drive and walked up to the house. The dogs were asleep, and hadn't heard them. When I went indoors to get a beer, I found them in the sitting-room, chatting to each other as they examined the books and the furniture. I was startled. They weren't.

'Ah, there you are,' said the husband. 'We read the bits in *The Sunday Times*, so we decided to pop in.'

That was it. No excuses, no hint of awkwardness, no thought that I might not be thrilled to see them. They didn't even have a copy of the book. Waiting for the paperback to come out, they said. Hardcover books are so expensive these days. They oozed an unfortunate mixture of familiarity and condescension.

It is not often that I take against people on sight, but I took against them. I asked them to leave.

The husband's red wattles turned even redder, and he puffed up like an aggrieved turkey who had just been told the bad news about Christmas.

'But we've driven all the way over from St Rémy.' I asked him to drive all the way back, and they left in a cloud of muttering. That's *one* book we won't be buying, only wanted to *look*, anyone would think it was Buckingham Palace. I watched them march down the drive to their Volvo, shoulders rigid with indignation, and thought about getting a Rottweiler.

After that, the sight of a car slowing down and stopping on the road in front of the house was the signal for what came to be known as a crawler alert. 'Make yourself decent,' my wife would say, 'I think they're coming up the drive. No – they've stopped at the mailbox.' And later on, when I went down to collect the post, there was a copy of the book in a plastic bag, to be signed and left under a stone on top of the well. The next day it was gone; taken, I hoped, by the considerate people who had delivered it without wanting to disturb us.

By the end of summer, we were not the only ones to have received some attention from the public. Our neighbour Faustin had been asked to autograph a book, which had puzzled him since, as he said, he was not an *écrivang*. When I told him that people had been reading about him in England, he took off his cap and smoothed his hair and said *Ah bon?* twice, sounding rather pleased.

Maurice the chef had also done his share of signing, and said he'd never had so many English customers in his restaurant. Some of them had been surprised to find that he actually existed; they thought I'd made him up. Others had arrived with copies of the book and had ordered, down to the final glass of *marc*, a meal that they had read about.

And then there was the celebrity plumber, Monsieur Menicucci, who drops in from time to time between his *œuvres* to share with us his thoughts on politics, wild mushrooms, climatic irregularities, the prospects for the French rugby team, the genius of Mozart and any exciting developments in the world of sanitary fittings. I gave him a copy of the book and showed him passages in which he had starred, and told him that some of our visitors had expressed a desire to meet him.

He adjusted his woollen bonnet and straightened the collar of his old check shirt. '*C'est vrai?*'

Yes, I said, absolutely true. His name had even appeared in *The Sunday Times*. Perhaps I should organize a signing session for him.

'*Ah, Monsieur Peter, vous rigolez.*' But I could see that he was not displeased at the idea, and he went off holding his book as carefully as if he were carrying a fragile and expensive bidet.

The voice on the other end of the phone could have come all the way from Sydney, cheerful and twangy.

'G'day. Wally Storer here, from the English Bookshop in Cannes; plenty of Poms down here, and your book's going nicely. How about coming along to sign a few copies one day during the Film Festival?'

I have always had doubts about the literary appetite of people in the film business. An old friend who works in Hollywood confessed that he had read one book in six years, and he was considered a borderline intellectual. If you mention Rimbaud in Bel Air it is assumed that you're talking about Sylvester Stallone. I didn't hold out much hope for writer's cramp and mammoth sales. Even so, I thought it would be fun. Maybe I'd see a star, or a topless sensation on the Croisette or – the rarest sight in town – a smiling waiter on the Carlton Hotel terrace. I said I'd be happy to come.

It was hot and sunny, bad weather for bookshops, as I joined the traffic crawling into town. Bright new signs on the lamp-posts announced that Cannes was twinned with Beverly Hills, and I could imagine the mayors finding endless excuses to exchange visits in the cause of municipal friendship and the shared interest of taking free holidays.

Outside the Palais des Festivals, what seemed to be the entire Cannes police force, equipped with revolvers, walkie-talkies and sunglasses, was busy creating a series of traffic jams and making sure Clint Eastwood didn't get kidnapped. With the skill that comes from many years of practice, they directed cars into snarling knots and then whistled at them furiously, sending the drivers off to the next snarling knot with irritated jerks of the head. It took me ten minutes to cover fifty yards. When I finally reached the vast underground car park, I saw that an earlier victim of the chaos had scrawled on the wall: 'Cannes is a great place to visit, but I wouldn't want to spend the day here.'

I went to a café on the Croisette to have breakfast and look for stars. Everyone else was doing the same thing. Never have so many unknowns inspected each other so carefully. All the girls were wearing pouts and trying to look bored. All the men carried listings of the films to be shown that day, and made important notes in the margins. One or two cordless phones were placed with casual prominence next to their croissants, and everyone displayed plastic delegates' badges and the obligatory Festival bag, with *Le Film Français/Cannes 90* printed on it. There was no mention of *Le Film Américain* or *Le Film Anglais*, but I suppose that's one of the advantages of being the host on these occasions; you get to choose the bags.

The Croisette was planted with a forest of posters carrying the names of actors, directors, producers and, for all I knew, hairdressers. They were positioned directly opposite the big hotels, presumably so that the hero of each poster could see his name every morning from his bedroom window before having the traditional Cannes breakfast of ham and ego. A feeling of hustle was in the air, of big deals and big bucks, and the groups of hustlers walking along the Croisette were oblivious to the old beggar sitting on the pavement outside the Hotel Majestic with a lonely 20-centime piece in his upturned, tattered hat.

Fortified by my dose of glamour, I left the moguls to it and went down the narrow Rue Bivouac-Napoléon to the English Bookshop, preparing for the odd experience of sitting in a shop window hoping for someone – anyone – to ask me to sign a book. I'd done one or two signings before. They were unnerving occasions when I had been stared at from a safe distance by people who were unwilling to venture within talking range. Perhaps they thought I'd bite. Little did they know the relief authors feel when a brave spirit approaches the table. After a few minutes of sitting on your own, you're ready to clutch at any straw and sign anything from books and photographs to old copies of *Nice-Matin* and cheques.

Fortunately, Wally Storer and his wife had anticipated author's funk and had stocked the shop with friends and customers. What inducements they had used to drag them off the beach I didn't know, but I was grateful to be kept busy, and I even started to wish I'd brought Monsieur Menicucci along. He would have answered much better than I why French drains behave and smell the way they do, which I found to be a topic of common curiosity among English expatriates. Isn't it strange, they said, that the French are so good at sophisticated technology like high-speed trains and electronic telephone systems and Concorde, and yet revert to the eighteenth century in their bathrooms. Only the other day, an elderly lady informed me, she had flushed her lavatory and the remains of a mixed salad had surfaced in the bowl. Really, it was *too bad*. That sort of thing would never happen in Cheltenham.

The signing came to an end, and we went round the corner to a bar. Americans and English outnumbered the natives, but natives in Cannes are few and far between. Even many of the police, I was told, are imported from Corsica.

They were still patrolling the Croisette when I left, toying with the traffic and eyeing the girls who sauntered by in varying stages of undress. The old beggar hadn't moved from his pitch in front of the Majestic, and his 20-centime piece was as lonely as ever. I dropped some coins in his hat and he told me, in English, to have a nice day. I wondered if he was practising for Beverly Hills.

7

Passing 50 Without Breaking the Speed Limit

I have never paid any great attention to my birthdays, even those which marked the accomplishment of having tottered through another ten years of life. I was working on the day I turned thirty, I was working on the day I turned forty, and I was quite happy at the thought of working on my fiftieth birthday. But it was not to be. Madame my wife had different ideas.

'You're going to be half a hundred,' she said. 'Considering the amount of wine you drink, that is some kind of achievement. We should celebrate.'

There is no arguing with her when she has a certain set to her chin, and so we talked about how and where the deed should be done. I might have known that my wife had already arranged it; she was listening to my suggestions – a trip to Aix, a *déjeuner flottant* in the pool, a day by the sea at Cassis – out of politeness. When I ran out of inspiration, she moved in. A picnic in the Lubéron, she said, with a few close friends. That was the way to celebrate a birthday in Provence. She painted lyrical pictures of a sun-dappled glade in the forest. I wouldn't even have to wear long trousers. I'd love it.

I couldn't imagine loving a picnic. My picnic experiences, limited as they had been to England, had left memories of rising damp creeping up the spine from permanently moist earth, of ants disputing with me over the food, of tepid white wine and of scuttling for shelter when the inevitable cloud arrived overhead and burst on top of us. I loathed picnics. Rather ungraciously, I said so.

This one, said my wife, would be different. She had it all worked out. In fact, she was in deep consultation with Maurice, and what she had in mind would be not only civilized but highly picturesque, an occasion to rival Glyndebourne on a dry day.

Maurice, the chef and owner of the Auberge de la Loube in Buoux and a serious horse-fancier, had over the years collected and restored two or three nineteenth-century *calèches*, or open carriages, and a horse-drawn limousine, a stagecoach, *une vraie diligence*. He was now offering his more adventurous clients the chance to trot to lunch. I would *love* it.

I recognize inevitability when it stares me in the face, and it was settled. We invited eight friends and kept our fingers crossed, less tightly than we would have done in England, for fine weather. Although it had rained only once since early April, two months before, June in Provence is unpredictable and sometimes wet.

But when I woke and went out into the courtyard, the seven o'clock sky was a never-ending blue, the colour of a Gauloise packet. The flagstones were warm under my bare feet, and our resident lizards had already taken up their sunbathing positions, flattened and motionless against the wall of the house. Just to get up to a morning like this was enough of a birthday present.

The beginning of a hot summer day in the Lubéron, sitting on the terrace with a bowl of *café crème*, the bees rummaging in the lavender and the light turning the forest to a dark burnished green, is better than waking up suddenly rich. Warmth gives me a sense of physical well-being and optimism; I didn't feel a day older than forty-nine, and looking down at ten brown toes I hoped I'd be doing exactly the same thing on my sixtieth birthday.

A little later, as warmth was turning into heat, the hum-buzz of the bees was blotted out by the clatter of a diesel engine, and I watched as a venerable open-top Land Rover, painted camouflage green, panted up the drive and stopped in a cloud of dust. It was Bennett, looking like the reconnais-sance scout from a Long Range Desert Group – shorts and shirt of military cut, tank commander sunglasses, vehicle festooned with jerricans and kitbags, face deeply tanned. Only the headgear, a Louis Vuitton baseball cap, would have been out of place at El Alamein. He had crossed enemy lines on the main N100 road, successfully invaded Ménerbes and was now ready for the final push into the mountains.

'My God, you're looking old,' he said, 'do you mind if I make a quick call? I left my swimming trunks at the house where I was staying last night. They're khaki, like General Noriega's underpants. Very unusual. I'd hate to lose them.'

While Bennett was on the phone, we rounded up our two house guests and three dogs and packed them in the car for the drive up to Buoux, where we were meeting the others. Bennett came out of the house and adjusted his baseball cap against the glare, and we set off in convoy, the Land Rover and its chauffeur attracting considerable interest from the peasants, waist-deep in the vines on either side of the road.

After Bonnieux, the scenery became wilder and harsher,

vines giving way to rock and scrub oak and purple-striped lavender fields. There were no cars and no houses. We could have been a hundred miles away from the chic villages of the Lubéron, and it pleased me to think that so much savage, empty country still existed. It would be a long time before there was a Souleiado boutique or a real estate agent's office up here.

We turned down into the deep valley. Buoux dozed. The dog who lives on the woodpile just past the *Mairie* opened one eye and barked perfunctorily, and a child holding a kitten looked up, small white saucers in a round brown face, at the unusual sight of traffic.

The area round the Auberge resembled a casting session for a film which had not quite decided on plot, characters, wardrobe or period. There was a white suit and a wide-brimmed Panama, there were shorts and espadrilles, a silk dress, a Mexican peon's outfit, scarves and bright shawls, hats of various colours and ages, one immaculately turned out baby and, leaping from his Land Rover to supervise kit inspection, our man from the desert.

Maurice appeared from the horses' parking area, smiling at us and the glorious weather. He was dressed in his Provençal Sunday best – white shirt and trousers, black bootlace tie, plum red waistcoat and an old flat straw hat. His friend, who was to drive the second carriage, was also in white, set off by thick crimson braces and a magnificent salt-and-pepper moustache, a dead ringer for Yves Montand in *Jean de Florette*.

'*Venez!*' said Maurice. 'Come and see the horses.' He led us through the garden, asking about the state of our appetites. The advance party had just left by van to set up the picnic, and there was a feast on board, enough to feed the whole of Buoux.

The horses were tethered in the shade, coats glossy, manes and tails coiffed. One of them whinnied and nosed at Maurice's waistcoat, looking for a sugar lump. The youngest guest, perched on her father's shoulders, gurgled at the sight of such a monster and leaned forward to poke one tentative pink finger into its shining chestnut flank. The horse mistook her for a fly, and whisked a long tail.

We watched as Maurice and Yves Montand hitched up the horses to the open *calèche*, black trimmed with red, and the seven-seater *diligence*, red trimmed with black – both of them oiled and waxed and buffed to a state of showroom finish. Maurice had spent all winter working on them and they were, as he said, '*impecc*'. The only modern addition was a vintage car horn the size and shape of a bugle, for use when overtaking less highly-tuned carriages, and to *éclater* any chickens who were thinking of crossing the road.

'*Allez! Montez!*'

We climbed in and moved off, observing the speed limit through the village. The dog on the woodpile barked goodbye, and we headed out into open country.

To travel in this way is to make you regret the invention of the car. There is a different view of everything, more commanding and somehow more interesting. There is a comfortable, swaying rhythm as the suspension adjusts to the gait of the horse and the changes of camber and surface. There is a pleasant background of old-fashioned noises as the harness creaks and the hooves clop and the steel rims of the wheels crunch the grit on the road. There is the *parfum* – a blend of warm horse, saddle soap, wood varnish and the smells of the fields that come to the nose unobstructed by windows. And there is the speed, or lack of it, which allows you time to *look*. In a car you're in a fast room. You see a blur, an impression;

you're insulated from the countryside. In a carriage, you're part of it.

'*Trottez!*' Maurice flicked the horse's rump with the whip and we changed into second gear. 'She's lazy, this one,' he said, 'and greedy. She goes more quickly on the way back, when she knows she will eat.' A long scarlet field, dense with poppies, unrolled slowly in the valley below us, and in the sky a buzzard wheeled and dipped, wings outstretched and still, balancing on air. As I watched it, a cloud covered the sun for a few moments and I could see the rays coming out behind it in dark, almost black spokes.

We turned off the road and followed a narrow track that twisted through the trees, and the sound of the horse's hooves was muffled by ragged, fragrant carpets of wild thyme. I asked Maurice how he found his picnic spots, and he told me that every week, on his day off, he had been exploring on horseback, sometimes riding for hours without meeting anyone.

'We're only twenty minutes from Apt,' he said, 'but nobody comes up here. Just me and the rabbits.'

The forest became thicker and the track narrower, barely wide enough for the carriage. Then we turned past an outcrop of rock, ducked through a tunnel of branches and there it was, spread out before us. Lunch.

'*Voilà!*' said Maurice. '*Le restaurant est ouvert.*'

At the end of a flat, grassy clearing, a table for ten had been set in the shade of a sprawling scrub oak – a table with a crisp white cloth, with ice buckets, with starched cotton napkins, with bowls of fresh flowers, with proper cutlery and proper chairs. Behind the table, a long-empty dry stone *borie* had been turned into a rustic bar, and I heard the pop of corks and clink of glasses. All my misgivings about picnics vanished. This was as far away from a damp bottom and ant sandwiches as one could possibly imagine.

Maurice roped off an area of the clearing and unhitched the horses, who rolled on their backs in the grass with the relief of two elderly ladies released from their corsets. The blinds of the *diligence* were drawn, and the youngest guest retired for a nap while the rest of us had a restorative glass of chilled peach champagne in the tiny open courtyard of the *borie*.

There is nothing like a comfortable adventure to put people in a good humour, and Maurice could hardly have hoped for a more appreciative audience. He deserved it. He had thought of everything, from an abundance of ice to toothpicks and, as he had said, there was no danger of us going hungry. He called us to sit down and gave us a guided tour of the first course: melon, quails' eggs, creamy *brandade* of cod, game *pâté*, stuffed tomatoes, marinated mushrooms – on and on it went, stretching from one end of the table to the other, looking, under the filtered sunlight, like an implausibly perfect still life from the pages of one of those art cookbooks that never sees the kitchen.

There was a short pause while I was presented with the heaviest and most accurate birthday card I had ever received – a round metal road sign, two feet in diameter, with a blunt reminder of the passing years in large black numerals. 50. *Bon anniversaire* and *bon appétit.*

We ate and drank like heroes, getting up in between courses, glasses in hand, to take recuperative strolls before coming back to the table for more. Lunch lasted nearly four hours, and by the time coffee and the birthday *gâteau* were served we had reached that state of contented inertia where even conversation is conducted in slow motion. The world was a rosy place. Fifty was a wonderful age.

The horses must have noticed the increased weight of their loads as they pulled out of the clearing towards the road that led back to Buoux, but they seemed more frisky than they had been in the morning, tossing their heads and testing the air through twitching nostrils. Sudden gusts of wind plucked at straw hats, and there was a growl of thunder. Within minutes, the blue sky turned black.

We had just reached the road when the hail started – pea-sized and painful, stinging the tops of our heads in the open *calèche* and bouncing off the broad wet back of the horse. She needed no encouragement from the whip. She was going full tilt, head down, body steaming. The brim of Maurice's straw hat had collapsed into bedraggled ears and his red waistcoat

was bleeding on to his trousers. He laughed, and shouted into the wind, '*Oh là là, le pique-nique Anglais!*'

My wife and I made a tent out of a travel blanket, and looked back to see how the *diligence* was dealing with the downpour. The top was obviously less weatherproof than it looked. Hands appeared from the side, tipping hatfuls of water overboard.

We came down into Buoux with Maurice braced, stiff-legged, hauling the reins tight against the headlong enthusiasm of the horse. She had scented home and food. To hell with humans and their picnics.

The sodden but cheerful storm victims gathered in the restaurant to be revived with tea and coffee and *marc*. Gone were the elegant picnickers of the morning, replaced by dripping, lank-haired figures dressed in varying degrees of transparency. Showing through a pair of once-white, once-opaque trousers, red-lettered knickers wished us all Merry Xmas. Clothes that had billowed now clung, and the straw hats looked like plates of congealed cornflakes. We each stood in our own private pools of water.

Madame and Marcel, the waiter, who had driven back in the van, served an assortment of dry clothes along with the *marc*, and the restaurant was transformed into a changing room. Bennett, pensive under his baseball cap, wondered if he might borrow a pair of swimming trunks for the drive home; the Land Rover was awash, and the driver's seat a puddle. But at least, he said, looking out of the window, the storm was over.

If it was over in Buoux, it had never happened in Ménerbes. The drive up to the house was still dusty, the grass was still brown, the courtyard still hot. We watched the sun as it balanced for a moment in the notch of the twin peaks to the west of the house before disappearing beneath a flushed sky.

'Well,' said my wife, 'now do you like picnics?'

What a question. Of course I like picnics. I love picnics.

8

The Flic

It was bad luck that I had no change for the parking meter on one of the few days that the Cavaillon traffic control authorities were out in force. There are two of them, well-padded and slow-moving men who do their best to look sinister in their peaked caps and sunglasses as they move with immense deliberation from car to car, looking for a *contravention*.

I had found a vacant meter that needed feeding, and I went into a nearby café for some 1-franc pieces. When I returned to the car, a portly figure in blue was squinting suspiciously at the dial on the meter. He looked up and aimed his sunglasses at me, tapping the dial with his pen.

'He has expired.'

I explained my problem, but he was not in the mood to consider any mitigating circumstances.

'*Tant pis pour vous*,' he said. '*C'est une contravention*.'

I looked around and could see that there were half a dozen cars double-parked. A *maçon*'s truck, brimming with rubble, was abandoned at the corner of a side street, completely blocking the exit. A van on the other side of the road had been left straddling a pedestrian crossing. My crime seemed relatively minor compared with these flagrant abuses, and I was unwise enough to say so.

I then became officially invisible. There was no reply except a sniff of irritation, and the guardian of the highways walked around me so that he could take down the number of the car. He unsheathed his notebook and consulted his watch.

He was starting to commit my sins to paper – probably adding on a bonus fine for impertinence – when there was a bawl from the café where I had been for change.

'*Eh, toi! Georges!*'

Georges and I looked round to see a stocky man making his way through the tables and chairs on the pavement, one finger wagging from side to side in the Provençal shorthand that expresses violent disagreement.

For five minutes, Georges and the stocky man shrugged and gesticulated and tapped each other sternly on the chest while my case was discussed. It was true, said the newcomer. Monsieur had just arrived, and he had indeed been into the café to get change. There were witnesses. He flung his arm back towards the café, where three or four faces were turned towards us from the twilight of the bar.

The law is the law, said Georges. It is a clear *contravention*. Besides, I have started to write the form, and so nothing can be done. It is irrevocable.

Mais c'est de la connerie, ça. Change the form, and give it to that woodenhead who is blocking the street with his truck.

Georges weakened. He looked at the truck and his note-book, gave another sniff, and turned to me so that he could have the last word. 'Next time, have change.' He looked at me intently, no doubt committing my criminal features to memory in case he might need to pull in a suspect one day, and moved off along the pavement towards the *maçon*'s truck.

My rescuer grinned and shook his head. 'He has *pois chiches* for brains, that one.'

I thanked him. Could I buy him a drink? We went into the café together and sat at a dark table in the corner, and I was there for the next two hours.

Robert was his name. He was not quite short, not quite fat, broad across the chest and stomach, thick-necked, dark-faced, dashingly moustached. His smile was a contrast in gold fillings and nicotine-edged teeth, and his brown eyes were lively with amusement. There was an air of faintly unreliable charm about him, the charm of an engaging scamp. I could imagine him in Cavaillon market selling guaranteed indestructible crockery and almost genuine Levi's, whatever might have fallen off the back of the *camion* the night before.

As it turned out, he had been a policeman, which was how he had come to know and dislike Georges. Now he was a security consultant, selling alarm systems to owners of second homes in the Lubéron. *Cambrioleurs* were everywhere nowadays, he said, looking for the open window or the unlocked door. It was wonderful for business. Did I have an alarm system? No? *Quelle horreur!* He slipped a card across the table. There was his name and a slogan that read Alarm Technology of the Future, a message that was somewhat at odds with his trademark – a small drawing of a parrot on a perch squawking '*Au voleur!*'

I was interested in his work with the police, and why he had left. He settled back in a cloud of Gitanes smoke, waved his empty glass at the barman for more *pastis*, and started to talk.

In the beginning, he said, it had been a little slow. Waiting for promotion, just like everyone else, trudging through the routine work, getting bored with the desk jobs, not the kind of excitement he had hoped for. And then came the break, one weekend in Fréjus, where he was taking a few days' leave.

Every morning he went for breakfast to a café overlooking the sea, and every morning at the same time a man came down to the beach for windsurfing lessons. With the idle half-interest of a holidaymaker, Robert watched as the man got up on his windsurfer, fell off and got up again.

There was something familiar about the man. Robert had never met him, he was sure, but he had seen him somewhere. There was a prominent mole on his neck, a tattoo on his left arm, the kind of small distinguishing marks that a policeman is trained to notice and remember. It was the windsurfer's profile that stirred Robert's memory, the mole on the neck and the slightly hooked nose.

After two days, it came to him. He had seen the profile, in black and white with a number underneath it; an identity photograph, a police mug shot. The windsurfer had a record.

Robert went to the local *gendarmerie*, and within half an hour he was looking at the face of a man who had escaped from prison the year before. He was the leader of *le gang de Gardanne*, and known to be dangerous. Physical characteristics included a mole on the neck and a tattoo on the left arm.

A trap was set, which Robert described with some difficulty through his laughter. Twenty officers, disguised in swimming trunks, appeared on the beach bright and early and attempted to look inconspicuous despite the curious similarity of their *bronzage* – the policeman's suntan of brown forearms, brown vee at the neck and brown face, with everywhere else, from toes to forehead, an unweathered white.

Fortunately, the fugitive was too busy getting aboard his windsurfer to notice anything suspicious about twenty pale men loitering with intent until they surrounded him in shallow water and took him away. A subsequent search of his studio apartment in Fréjus produced two Magnum 357 handguns and three grenades.

Robert was credited with the collar, and seconded to plain-clothes duty at Marignane airport, where his powers of observation could be fully exploited.

I stopped him there for a moment, because I had always been puzzled by the apparent lack of official surveillance at Marseille. Arriving passengers can leave their hand luggage with friends while they go to the baggage claim area, and if all they have is hand luggage they don't need to pass through Customs at all. Given Marseille's reputation, this seemed strangely casual.

Robert tilted his head and laid a stubby finger along the side of his nose. It is not quite as *décontracté* as it appears, he said. Police and *douaniers*, sometimes dressed as business executives, sometimes in jeans and T-shirts, are always there, mingling with the passengers, strolling through the parking areas, watching and listening. He himself had caught one or two petty smugglers – nothing big, just amateurs who thought that once they were in the car park they'd be safe, they could slap each other on the back and talk about it. Crazy.

But there were weeks when nothing much happened, and in the end boredom had got to him. That, and his *zizi*. He grinned, and pointed with his thumb down between his legs.

He'd stopped a girl – a good-looking girl, well-dressed, travelling alone, the classic drug 'mule' – as she was getting into a car with Swiss plates. He asked her the standard question, how long the car had been in France. She became nervous, then friendly, then very friendly, and the two of them had spent the afternoon together in the airport hotel. Robert had been seen coming out with her, and that was it. *Fini*. Funnily enough, it had been the same week that a warden in Marseille's Beaumettes jail had been caught passing Scotch in doctored yogurt pots to one of the prisoners. *Fini* for him too.

Robert shrugged. It was wrong, it was stupid, but policemen weren't saints. There were always the *brebis galeuses*, the black sheep. He looked down at his glass, the picture of a penitent man regretting past misdeeds. One slip, and a career in ruins. I started to feel sorry for him, and said so. He reached across the table and patted my arm, and then spoiled the effect by saying that another drink would make him feel much better. He laughed, and I wondered how much of what he'd told me was the truth.

In a moment of *pastis*-scented *bonhomie*, Robert had said that he would come up to the house one day to advise us on our security arrangements. There would be no obligation, and if we should decide to make ourselves impregnable, he would install the most technically advanced booby traps at a *prix d'ami*.

I thanked him and forgot about it. Favours offered in bars should never be taken too seriously, particularly in Provence, where the most sober of promises is likely to take months to materialize. In any case, having seen how carefully members of the public ignore the shriek of car alarm systems in the

streets, I was not convinced that electronic devices were much of a deterrent. I had more faith in a barking dog.

To my surprise, Robert came as he said he would, in a silver BMW a-bristle with antennae, dressed in perilously tight trousers and a black shirt, humming with a musky and aggressive after-shave. The splendour of his appearance was explained by his companion, whom he introduced as his friend Isabelle. They were going to have lunch in Gordes, and Robert thought it was a chance to combine business with pleasure. He managed to make it sound infinitely suggestive.

Isabelle was no more than twenty. A blonde fringe brushed the rims of gigantic sunglasses. A minimal part of her body was coated with hot-pink spandex, an iridescent tube which ended well above mid-thigh. The courtly Robert insisted that she lead the way up the steps to the house, and he clearly relished every step. He was a man who could give lessons in leering.

While Isabelle busied herself with the contents of her make-up bag, I took Robert round the house, and he gave me a predictably disturbing assessment of the opportunities that our home provided for any larcenous idiot with a screw-driver. Windows and doors and shutters were all inspected and dismissed as being next to useless. And the dogs? *Aucun problème*. They could be taken care of with a few scraps of drugged meat, and then the house would be at the mercy of the thieves. Robert's overwhelming after-shave gusted over me as he pinned me against the wall. *You have no idea what these animals do.*

His voice became low and confidential. He wouldn't want Madame my wife to overhear what he was about to tell me, since it was rather indelicate.

Burglars, he said, are often superstitious. In many cases –
he had seen it more times than he liked to think about – they
feel it necessary before leaving a ransacked house to defecate,
usually on the floor, preferably on fitted carpet. In this way,
they think that any bad luck will remain in the house
instead of with them. *Merde partout*, he said, and made the
word sound as if he'd just stepped in it. *C'est désagréable, non?*
It certainly was. *Désagréable* was a mild way of putting it.

But, said Robert, life was sometimes just. An entire group
of *cambrioleurs* had once been apprehended because of this
very superstition. The house had been picked clean, the
swag loaded into a truck, and all that remained was to
perform the parting gesture, for good luck's sake. The head
of the gang, however, experienced considerable difficulty in
making his contribution. Try as he might, nothing happened.
He was *très, très constipé*. And he was still there, crouched
and cursing, when the police arrived.

It was a heartening story, although I realized that according to the national average we had only a one in five chance
of being visited by a constipated burglar. We couldn't count
on it.

Robert took me outside and began to propose his plans for
turning the house into a fortress. At the bottom of the drive,
there should be electronically operated steel gates. In front of
the house, a pressure-activated lighting system; anything
heavier than a chicken coming up the drive would be caught
in the glare of a battery of floodlights. This was often enough
to make burglars give up and run for it. But to be totally
protected, to be able to sleep like an innocent child, one
should also have the last word in repellents – *la maison
hurlante*, the howling house.

Robert paused to gauge my reaction to this hideous

novelty, and smiled across at Isabelle, who was peering over her sunglasses at her nails. They were a perfect hot-pink match for her dress.

'*Ça va, chou-chou?*'

She twitched a honey-coloured shoulder at him, and it was with a visible effort that he turned his thoughts back to howling houses.

Alors, it was all done with electronic beams, which protected every door, every window, every orifice larger than a chink. And so if a determined and light-footed burglar managed to scale the steel gates and tiptoe through the floodlights, the merest touch of his finger on window or door would set the house screaming. One could also, *bien sûr*, enhance the effect by installing an amplifier on the roof so that the screams could be heard for several kilometres.

But that wasn't the end of it. At the same time, a partner of Robert's near Gordes, whose house was linked to the system, would drive over instantly with his loaded *pistolet* and his large Alsatian. Secure behind this multi-layered protection, I would be perfectly *tranquille*.

It sounded anything but *tranquille*. I immediately thought of Faustin in his tractor, pounding on the steel gates at six in the morning to get to the vines; of the floodlights going on all through the night as foxes or *sangliers* or the cat next door crossed the drive; of setting off the howling mechanism by accident, and having to apologize fast to an irritated man with a gun before his dog ripped me to pieces. Life in Fort Knox would be a permanent, dangerous hell. Even as a barricade against the August invasion, it simply wouldn't be worth the nervous wear and tear.

Luckily, Robert was distracted from pressing for a sale. Isabelle, now satisfied with the state of her nails, the positioning of her sunglasses and the overall adhesion of her tubelet, was ready to go. She cooed across the courtyard at him. '*Bobo, j'ai faim.*'

'*Oui, oui, chérie. Deux secondes.*' He turned to me and tried to revert to business, but his howling mechanism had been activated and our domestic security was not the pressing priority of the moment.

I asked him where he was going to have lunch.

'*La Bastide,*' he said. 'Do you know it? It used to be the *gendarmerie*. Once a *flic*, always a *flic*, eh?'

I said I'd heard that it was also an hotel, and he winked. He was a very expressive winker. This was a wink of the purest lubricity.

'I know,' he said.

9

Mouthful for Mouthful with the Athlete Gourmet

We heard about Régis from some friends. They had invited him to dinner at their house, and during the morning he had called to ask what he would be given to eat. Even in France, that shows a greater interest than normal in the menu, and his hostess was curious. Why was he asking? There were cold stuffed *moules*, there was pork with truffle gravy, there were cheeses, there were home-made sorbets. Were any of these a problem? Had he developed allergies? Become a vegetarian? Gone, God forbid, on a diet?

Certainly not, said Régis. It all sounded delicious. But there was *un petit inconvénient*, and it was this: he was suffering from a sharp attack of piles, and found it impossible to sit through an entire dinner. A single course was all that he could manage without discomfort, and he wanted to pick the course which tempted him most. He was sure that his hostess would sympathize with his predicament.

As it was Régis, she did. Régis, so she told us later, was a man whose life was dedicated to the table – knowledgeably, almost obsessively concerned with eating and drinking. But not as a glutton. No, Régis was a gourmet who happened to have a huge and extremely well-informed appetite. Also, she said, he was amusing about his passion, and he had some views which we might find interesting about the English attitude to food. Perhaps we would like to meet him once he had recovered from his *crise postérieure*.

And, one evening a few weeks later, we did.

He arrived in haste, nursing a cold bottle of Krug champagne, not quite cold enough, and spent the first five minutes fussing with an ice bucket to bring the bottle to the correct drinking temperature, which he said had to be between 5 and 7 degrees. While he rotated the bottle gently in the bucket, he told us of a dinner party he had been to the previous week which had been a gastronomic disaster. His only enjoyable moment, he said, had come at the end, when one of the female guests was saying goodbye to her hostess.

'What an unusual evening,' she had said. 'Everything was cold except the champagne.'

Régis quivered with laughter and eased the cork out so carefully that there was nothing but a quiet, effervescent sigh to mark the opening.

He was a large man, dark and fleshy, with the deep blue eyes that are sometimes found, rather surprisingly, in swarthy Provençal faces. Unlike the rest of us in our conventional clothes, he was dressed in a tracksuit – pale grey, trimmed in red, with *Le Coq Sportif* embroidered on the chest. His shoes were equally athletic – complicated creations with multi-coloured layers of rubber sole, more suitable for a marathon than an evening under the dinner table. He saw me looking at them.

'I must be comfortable when I eat,' he said, 'and nothing is more comfortable than the clothing of athletes. Also . . .' he pulled his waistband in and out '. . . one can make a place for the second helping. *Très important*.' He grinned, and raised his glass. 'To England and the English, as long as they keep their cooking to themselves.'

Most of the French people we had met were more or less disdainful of *la cuisine Anglaise* without knowing very much about it. But Régis was different. He had made a study of the English and their eating habits, and during dinner he told us exactly where we went wrong.

It starts, he said, at babyhood. The English baby is fed on bland mush, the kind of pabulum one would give to an undiscriminating chicken, *sans caractère, sans goût*. The French infant, however, even before he has teeth, is treated as a human being with taste buds. As evidence, Régis described the menu offered by Gallia, one of the leading baby food manufacturers. It included brains, fillet of sole, *poulet au riz*, tuna, lamb, liver, veal, gruyère, soups, fruits, vegetables, puddings of quince and bilberry, *crème caramel* and *fromage blanc*. All of that and more, said Régis, before the child is eighteen months old. You see? The palate is being educated. He paused to lower his head over the chicken in tarragon that had just been put in front of him, inhaled, and adjusted the napkin tucked in the collar of his tracksuit.

He then moved on a few years to the point where the budding gourmet goes to school. Did I remember, he asked me, the food I ate at school? I did indeed, with horror, and he nodded understandingly. English school food, he said, is famously horrible. It is grey and *triste* and mysterious, because you never know what it is you're trying to force yourself to eat. But at the village school attended by his five-year-old daughter, the menu for the week is posted on the notice board, so that meals won't be duplicated at home, and each day there is a three-course lunch. Yesterday, for instance, little Mathilde had eaten a celery salad with a slice of ham and cheese *quiche, riz aux saucisses* and baked bananas. *Voilà!* The palate continues its education. And so it is inevitable that the French adult has a better appreciation of food, and higher expectations, than the English adult.

Régis sliced a fat pear to eat with his cheese, and pointed his knife at me as if I had been responsible for the badly educated English palate. We now come, he said, to restaurants. He shook his head sorrowfully, and placed his hands wide apart on the table, palms upwards, fingers bunched together. Here – the left hand was raised a couple of inches – you have *le pub*. Picturesque, but with food only as a sponge for beer. And here – the other hand was raised higher – you have expensive restaurants for *hommes d'affaires* whose companies pay for what they eat.

And in the middle? Régis looked at the space between his two hands, the corners of his mouth turned down, an expression of despair on his plump face. In the middle is a desert, *rien*. Where are your *bistrots*? Where are your honest *bourgeois* restaurants? Where are your *relais routiers*? Who but a rich man can afford to go out and eat well in England?

I would have liked to argue with him, but I didn't have the ammunition. He was asking questions that we had asked ourselves many times when we were living in the country in England, where the choice was limited to pubs or tarted-up restaurants with delusions of adequacy and London-sized bills. In the end, we had given up, defeated by microwaved specialities and table wine served in ceremonial baskets by charming but incompetent people called Justin or Emma.

Régis stirred his coffee and hesitated for a moment between Calvados and the tall, frosted bottle of *eau de vie de poires* from Manguin in Avignon. I asked him about his favourite restaurants.

'There is always Les Baux,' he said. 'But the bill is spectacular.' He shook his hand from the wrist as if he had burnt his fingers. 'It is not for every day. In any case, I prefer places more modest, less international.'

In other words, I said, more French.

'*Voilà!*' said Régis. 'More French, and where one finds a *rapport qualité-prix*, a value for money. That still exists here, you know, at every level. I have made a study of it.'

I was sure he had, but he still hadn't given me any names apart from Les Baux, which we were saving until we won the national lottery. How about something a little less grand?

'If you like,' said Régis, 'it would be amusing to have lunch at two restaurants, very different, but both of a high standard.' He poured another nip of Calvados – 'for the digestion' – and leaned back in his chair. 'Yes,' he said, 'it will be my contribution to the education of *les Anglais*. Your wife will come, *naturellement*.' Of course she would come. The wife of Régis, unfortunately, would not be with us. She would be at home, preparing dinner.

He told us to meet him in Avignon, at one of the cafés in the Place de l'Horloge, when he would reveal the first of his two chosen restaurants. He kissed his fingers noisily over the phone, and advised us not to make any arrangements for the afternoon. After a lunch such as the one he planned, nothing more energetic than a *digestif* would be possible.

We watched him as he billowed towards us across the *place*, moving lightly for such a big man in his black basketball boots and what must have been his formal tracksuit, also black, with UCLA in pink letters on one meaty thigh. He was carrying a shopping basket and a zip-striped handbag of the kind that French executives use for their personal documents and emergency bottles of *eau de cologne.*

He ordered a glass of champagne and showed us some baby melons, no bigger than apples, that he had just bought in the market. They were to be scooped clean, dosed with a ratafia of grape juice and brandy and left for twenty-four hours in the refrigerator. They would taste, so Régis assured us, like a young girl's lips. I had never thought of melons in quite that way before, but I put that down to the short-comings of my English education.

With a final fond squeeze of their tiny green bottoms, Régis put the melons back in the basket and addressed himself to the business of the day.

'We are going,' he said, 'to Hiély, just over there in the Rue de la République. Pierre Hiély is a prince of the kitchen. He has been at the ovens for twenty, twenty-five years, and he is a prodigy. Never a disappointing meal.' Régis wagged his finger at us. '*Jamais!*'

Apart from a small framed menu at the entrance, Hiély makes no attempt to entice the passer-by. The narrow door opens into a narrow corridor, and the restaurant is up a flight of stairs. It's a big room with a handsome herringbone parquet floor, decorated in sober colours, tables spaced comfortably far apart. Here, as in most good French restaurants, the solitary client is treated as well as a party of half a dozen. Tables for one are not wedged into a dead corner as an afterthought, but in windowed alcoves overlooking the street. These were already occupied by men in suits, presumably local businessmen who had to snatch their lunch in a mere two hours before going back to the office. The other clients, all French except for us, were less formally dressed.

I remembered being turned away from a restaurant with

airs and graces in Somerset because I wasn't wearing a tie, something that has never happened to me in France. And here was Régis, resembling a refugee from the weight-watchers' gym in his tracksuit, being welcomed like a king by Madame as he checked in his shopping basket and asked if Monsieur Hiély was on form. Madame allowed herself a smile. '*Oui, comme toujours.*'

Régis beamed and rubbed his hands together as we were shown to our table, sniffing the air to see if he could pick up any hints of what was to come. In another of his favourite restaurants, he said, the chef allowed him into the kitchen, and he would close his eyes and select his meal by nose.

He tucked his napkin under his chin and murmured to the waiter. '*Un grand?*' said the waiter. '*Un grand,*' said Régis, and sixty seconds later a large glass pitcher, opaque with cold, was placed in front of us. Régis became professorial; our lesson was about to commence. 'In a serious restaurant,' he said, 'one can always have confidence in the house wines. This is a Côtes-du-Rhône. *Santé.*' He took a gargantuan sip and chewed on it for a few seconds before expressing his satisfaction with a sigh.

'*Bon.* Now, you will permit some advice on the menu? As you see, there is a *dégustation* which is delicious, but possibly a little long for a simple lunch. There is a fine choice *à la carte*. But we must remember why we are here.' He looked at us over the top of his wine glass. 'It is so that you can experience the *rapport qualité-prix*. Any good chef can feed you well for 500 francs a head. The test is how well you can eat for less than half that, and so I propose the short menu. *D'accord?*'

We were *d'accord*. The short menu was enough to make a Michelin inspector salivate, let alone two English amateurs like us. With some difficulty, we made our decisions while Régis hummed quietly over the wine list. He beckoned over the waiter for another reverent exchange of murmurs.

'I break my own rule,' said Régis. 'The red house wine is, of course, faultless. But here,' he tapped the page in front of him, 'here is a little treasure, *pas cher*, from the Domaine de Trévallon, north of Aix. Not too heavy, but with the character of a big wine. You will see.'

As one waiter departed for the cellar, another arrived with a snack to keep us going until the first course was ready – small ramekins, each filled with a creamy *brandade* of cod, topped with a tiny, perfectly fried quail's egg and garnished with black olives. Régis was silent with concentration, and I could hear the moist creak of corks being eased from bottles, the low voices of the waiters and the subdued chink of knives and forks against thin china plates.

Régis wiped his ramekin clean with a scrap of bread – he used bread like an implement to guide food to his fork – and poured some more wine. '*Ça commence bien, eh?*'

And lunch continued as it had begun, *bien*. A flan of *foie gras* in a thick but delicate sauce of wild mushrooms and asparagus was followed by home-made sausages of Sisteron lamb and sage with a *confiture* of sweet red onions and, in a separate flat dish, a gratin of potato that was no thicker than my napkin, a single crisp layer which dissolved on the tongue.

Now that the edge was off his appetite, Régis was able to resume conversation, and he told us about a literary project that he was considering. He had read in the paper that an international centre for Marquis de Sade studies was to be opened during the Avignon festival. There would also be an opera performed in honour of *le divin marquis*, and a champagne named after him. These events indicated a renewal of public interest in the old monster and, as Régis pointed out, even sadists have to eat. His idea was to give them their very own recipes.

'I shall call it *Cuisine Sadique: The Marquis de Sade's Cookbook*,' he said, 'and all the ingredients will be beaten, whipped, trussed, crushed or seared. There will be many painful words used in the descriptions and so I am sure it will be a *succès fou* in Germany. But you must advise me about England.' He leaned forward and his voice became confidential. 'Is it true that all men who have been to English public schools are fond of . . . *comment dirais-je* . . . a little punishment?' He sipped his wine and raised his eyebrows. '*Le spanking, non?*'

I said that he should try to find a publisher who had been to Eton, and to devise a recipe which included flogging.

'*Qu'est-ce que ça veut dire*, flogging?'

I explained as best I could, and Régis nodded. '*Ah, oui.* Maybe with a breast of chicken one could do flogging, with a very sharp sauce of *citron*. *Très bien*.' He made notes in a small, neat hand on the back of his cheque book. '*Un best-seller, c'est certain.*'

The best-seller was put aside while Régis took us on a tour of the cheese trolley, stopping frequently *en route* to instruct us and the waiter on the correct balance between hard and soft, *piquant* and *doux*, fresh and aged. He chose five out of the twenty or more cheeses on offer, and congratulated himself on having had the foresight to predict that we would need a second bottle of Trévallon.

I bit into a peppery goat's cheese, and felt a prickle of perspiration on the bridge of my nose under my glasses. The wine slipped down like silk. It had been a wonderful meal, completely satisfying, served with easy efficiency by highly professional waiters. I told Régis how much I had enjoyed it, and he looked at me with surprise.

'But we haven't finished. There is more.' A plate of tiny meringues was put on the table. 'Ah,' he said, 'these are to help us prepare for the desserts. They taste like clouds.' He ate two in quick succession, and looked round to make sure the dessert waiter hadn't forgotten us.

A second vehicle, larger and more loaded than the cheese trolley, was wheeled carefully up to the table and parked in front of us. It would have caused deep distress to anyone with a weight problem: bowls of fresh cream and *fromage blanc*, truffled chocolate cake covered in more chocolate, pastries, *vacherins*, rum-soaked *babas*, tarts, sorbets, *fraises des bois*, fruits bathed in syrup – it was all too much for Régis to take in while sitting down, and so he got up and prowled around to make sure that nothing was hiding behind the fresh raspberries.

My wife chose ice cream made with local honey, and the waiter took a spoon from its pot of hot water, scooping the ice cream from the bowl with a graceful roll of the wrist. He stood with plate and spoon, poised for further instructions. '*Avec ça?*'

'*C'est tout, merci.*'

Régis made up for my wife's restraint with what he called a selection of textures – chocolate, pastry, fruit and cream – and pushed the sleeves of his tracksuit up above his elbows. Even on him, the pace was beginning to tell.

I ordered coffee. There was a moment of shocked silence while Régis and the waiter looked at me.

'*Pas de dessert?*' said the waiter.

'It's part of the menu,' said Régis.

Both of them seemed worried, as though I had suddenly been taken ill, but it was no good. Hiély had won by a knock-out.

The bill was 230 francs a head, plus wine. It was astonishing value for money. For 280 francs, we could have had the long *menu dégustation*. Maybe next time, said Régis. Yes, maybe next time, after three days of fasting and a ten-mile walk.

The second half of the gastronomy course was postponed to allow Régis to take his annual cure. For two weeks, he ate sparingly – three-course meals instead of his customary five courses – and soaked his liver in mineral water. This was essential for the rejuvenation of his system.

To celebrate the end of the *régime*, he proposed lunch at a restaurant called *Le Bec Fin*, and told me to meet him there no later than quarter to twelve to be sure of a table. I should be able to find it easily enough, he said. It was on the RN 7 at Orgon, recognizable by the number of trucks in the car park. It would not be necessary to wear a jacket. My wife, wiser than I in the heat, decided to stay at home and guard the pool.

By the time I arrived, the restaurant was completely surrounded by trucks, their cabins jammed tight against tree trunks to take advantage of the scraps of shade. Half a dozen car transporters were drawn up, nose to tail, on the hard shoulder opposite. A latecomer cruised off the road, squeezed into a narrow strip next to the dining-room, and stopped with a hydraulic hiss of relief. The driver stood for a moment in the sun and eased his back, the shape of his arched spine repeated exactly in the generous swell of his stomach.

The bar was full and loud; big men, big moustaches, big bellies, big voices. Régis, standing in a corner with a glass, looked almost svelte by comparison. He was dressed for July, in running shorts and a sleeveless vest, his handbag looped over one wrist.

'*Salut!*' He tidied up the last of his *pastis* and ordered two more. '*C'est autre chose, eh? Pas comme Hiély.*'

It could hardly have been less like Hiély. Behind the bar, damp from the wet cloth that Madame was using in great swoops, was a notice that said *DANGER! RISQUE D'ENGUEULADE!* – watch out for a slanging match. Through the open door that led to the lavatory I could see another notice: *Douche, 8 francs.* From an invisible kitchen came the clatter of saucepans and the hot tang of simmering garlic.

I asked Régis how he felt after his period of self-imposed restraint, and he turned sideways to show off his belly in profile. Madame behind the bar looked up as she flicked the froth from a glass of beer with a wooden spatula. She inspected the long curve that started just below Régis's chest and ended overhanging the waistband of his running shorts. 'When's it due?' she asked.

We went through to the dining-room and found an empty table at the back. A small dark woman with a pretty smile and an undisciplined black brassière strap that resisted her efforts at adjustment came to tell us the rules. For the first course, we should serve ourselves from the buffet, and then there was a choice of beef, calamari or *poulet fermier*. The wine list was brief – red or *rosé*, which came in a litre bottle with a plastic stopper and a bowl of ice cubes. The waitress wished us *bon appétit*, performed a little bob that was almost a curtsey, hitched up her bra strap and went off with our order.

Régis opened the wine with mock ceremony and sniffed the plastic stopper. 'From the Var,' he said, '*sans prétention, mais honnête.*' He took a sip and drew it slowly through his front teeth. '*Il est bon.*'

We joined the line of truck-drivers at the buffet. They were achieving small miracles of balance, piling their plates with an assortment that was a meal in itself: two kinds of *saucisson*, hard-boiled eggs in mayonnaise, moist tangles of *céleri rémoulade*, saffron-coloured rice with red peppers, tiny peas and sliced carrots, a pork *terrine* in pastry, *rillettes*, cold squid, wedges of fresh melon. Régis grumbled at the size of the plates and took two, resting the second with a waiter's expertise on the inside of his forearm as he plundered each of the serving bowls.

There was a moment of panic when we returned to the table. Impossible even to think of eating without bread. Where was the bread? Régis caught the eye of our waitress and raised a hand to his mouth, making biting motions with bunched fingers against his thumb. She pulled a *baguette* from the brown paper sack standing in the corner and ran it through the guillotine with a speed that made me wince. The slices of bread were still reflating after the pressure of the blade when they were put in front of us.

I told Régis that he might be able to use the bread guillotine in his Marquis de Sade cookbook, and he paused in mid-*saucisson*.

'*Peut-être*,' he said, 'but one must be careful, above all with the American market. Have you heard about the difficulty with the champagne?'

Apparently, so Régis had read in a newspaper article, the champagne of the Marquis de Sade had not been welcome in the land of the free because of its label, which was decorated with a drawing of the top half of a well-endowed young woman. This might not have been a problem, except that a sharp-eyed guardian of public morality had noticed the position of the young woman's arms. It was not explicit, not depicted on the label itself, but there was the merest hint of a suggestion that the arms *might have been pinioned.*

Oh là là. Imagine the effect of such degeneracy on the youth of the country, not to mention some of the more susceptible adults. The fabric of society would be ripped asunder, and there would be champagne and bondage parties all the way from Santa Barbara to Boston. God only knows what might happen in Connecticut.

Régis resumed eating, his paper napkin tucked in the top of his vest. At the next table, a man on his second course unbuttoned his shirt to let the air circulate, and revealed a stupendous mahogany paunch with a gold crucifix suspended neatly between furry bosoms. Very few people were picking at their food, and I wondered how they could manage to stay alert at the wheel of a fifty-ton truck all afternoon.

We wiped our empty plates with bread, and then wiped our knives and forks the same way. Our waitress came with three oval stainless steel dishes, burning hot. On the first were two halves of a chicken in gravy; on the second, tomatoes stuffed with garlic and parsley; on the third, tiny potatoes that had been roasted with herbs. Régis sniffed everything before serving me.

'What do the *routiers* in England eat?'

Two eggs, bacon, chips, sausages, baked beans, a fried slice, a pint of tea.

'No wine? No cheese? No desserts?'

I didn't think so, although my *routier* experience had been very limited. I said they might stop at a pub, but the law about drinking and driving was severe.

Régis poured some more wine. 'Here in France,' he said, 'I am told that one is permitted an *apéritif,* half a bottle of wine and a *digestif.'*

I said that I had read somewhere about the accident rate in France being higher than anywhere in Europe, and twice as high as America.

'That has nothing to do with alcohol,' said Régis. 'It is a question of national *esprit*. We are impatient, and we love speed. *Malheureusement*, not all of us are good drivers.' He mopped his plate and changed the conversation back to more comfortable ground.

'This is a high quality chicken, don't you think?' He picked up a bone from his plate and tested it between his teeth. 'Good strong bones. He has been raised properly, in the open air. The bones of an industrial chicken are like *papier-mâché*.'

It was indeed a fine chicken, firm but tender, and perfectly cooked, like the potatoes and the garlicky tomatoes. I said that I was surprised not only at the standard of cooking, but at the abundance of the portions. And I was sure the bill wasn't going to be painful.

Régis cleaned his knife and fork again, and signalled the waitress to bring cheese.

'It's simple,' he said. 'The *routier* is a good client, very faithful. He will always drive the extra fifty kilometres to eat well at a correct price, and he will tell other *routiers* that the restaurant is worth a detour. As long as the standard is maintained, there will never be empty tables.' He waved a forkful of Brie at the dining-room. '*Tu vois?*'

I looked around, and gave up counting, but there must have been close to 100 men eating, and maybe thirty more in the bar.

'It is a solid business. But if the chef becomes mean, or starts cheating, or the service is too slow, the *routiers* will go. Within a month, there will be nobody, a few tourists.'

There was a rumble outside, and the room became sunny as a truck pulled away from its place next to the window. Our neighbour with the crucifix put on his sunglasses to eat his dessert, a bowl of three different ice creams.

'*Glaces, crème caramel ou flan?*' The black bra strap was hitched into place, only to slip out again as the waitress cleared our table.

Régis ate his *crème caramel* with soft sucking sounds of enjoyment, and reached for the ice cream that he had ordered for me. I'd never make a *routier*. I didn't have the capacity.

It was still early, well before two, and the room was beginning to clear. Bills were being paid – huge fingers opening dainty little purses to take out carefully folded banknotes, the waitress bobbing and smiling and hitching as she brought change and wished the men *bonne route*.

We had double-strength coffee, black and scalding beneath its scum of brown bubbles, and Calvados in rotund little glasses. Régis tipped his glass until its rounded side touched the table and the gold liquid exactly reached the rim – the old way, he said, of judging a true measure.

The bill for us both was 140 francs. Like our lunch at Hiély, it was wonderful value for money, and I had only one regret as we went outside and felt the hammer of the sun. If I'd brought a towel, I could have had a shower.

'Well,' said Régis, 'that will hold me until tonight.' We shook hands, and he threatened me with a *bouillabaisse* in Marseille on our next educational outing.

I went back into the bar for some more coffee, and to see if I could rent a towel.

10

Sporting and Fashion Notes from the Ménerbes Dog Show

The Ménerbes stadium, a level field among the vines, is normally the setting for loud and enthusiastic matches played by the village football team. There might be a dozen cars parked under the pine trees, and supporters divide their attention between the game and their copious picnics. But for one day a year, usually the second Sunday in June, the *stade* is transformed. Bunting, in the Provençal blood and guts colours of red and yellow, is strung across the forest paths. An overgrown hollow is cleared to provide extra parking, and a screen of *canisse* is erected along the side of the road so that passers-by can't watch the proceedings without paying their 15-franc entrance fee. Because this is, after all, a major local event, a mixture of Cruft's and Ascot, the *Foire aux Chiens de Ménerbes*.

This year it started early and noisily. Just after seven, we were opening the doors and shutters and enjoying the one morning of the week when our neighbour's tractor stays in bed. The birds were singing, the sun was shining, the valley was still. Peace, perfect peace. And then, half a mile away over the hill, the *chef d'animation* began his loudspeaker trials with an electronic yelp that ricocheted through the mountains and must have woken up half the Lubéron.

'*Allo allo, un, deux, trois, bonjour Ménerbes!*' He paused to cough. It sounded like an avalanche. '*Bon,*' he said, '*ça marche.*' He turned the volume down a notch and tuned into Radio Monte Carlo. A quiet morning was out of the question.

We had decided to wait until the afternoon before going to the show. By then, the preliminary heats would be over, mongrels and dogs of dubious behaviour weeded out, a good lunch would have been had by all and the best noses in the business would be ready to do battle in the field trials.

On the stroke of noon, the loudspeaker went dead and the background chorus of barking was reduced to the occasional plaintive serenade of a hound expressing unrequited lust or boredom. The valley was otherwise silent. For two hours, dogs and everything else took second place to stomachs.

'*Tout le monde a bien mangé?*' bellowed the loudspeaker. The microphone amplified a half-suppressed belch. '*Bon. Alors, on recommence.*' We started off along the track that leads to the *stade*.

A shaded clearing above the car park had been taken over by an élite group of dealers who were selling specialist breeds, or hybrids, dogs of particular and valuable skills – trackers of the wild *sanglier*, hunters of rabbits, detectors of quail and woodcock. They were strung like a living necklace on chains beneath the trees, twitching in their sleep. Their owners looked like gypsies: slender, dark men with gold teeth flashing through dense black moustaches.

One of them noticed my wife admiring a wrinkled black-and-tan specimen who was scratching his ear lazily with a huge back paw. '*Il est beau, eh?*' said the owner, and shone his teeth at us. He bent down and took hold of a handful of loose skin behind the dog's head. 'He comes in his own *sac à main*. You can carry him home.' The dog raised his eyes in resignation at having been born with a coat several sizes too big, and his paw stopped in mid-scratch. My wife shook her head. 'We already have three dogs.' The man shrugged, and let the skin drop in heavy folds. 'Three, four – what's the difference?'

A little further along the track, the sales presentation became more sophisticated. On top of a hutch made from plywood and wire netting, a printed card announced: *Fox-terrier, imbattable aux lapins et aux truffes. Un vrai champion.* The champion, a short, stout brown and white dog, was snoring on his back, all four stumpy legs in the air. We barely slowed down, but it was enough for the owner. '*Il est beau, eh?*' He woke the dog up and lifted him from the hutch. '*Regardez!*' He put the dog on the ground and took a slice of sausage from the tin plate that was next to the empty wine bottle on the bonnet of his van.

'*Chose extraordinaire,*' he said. 'When these dogs are eating, nothing will distract them. They become *rigide*. You press the back of the head and the rear legs will rise into the air.' He put the sausage down, covered it with leaves and let the dog root for it, then placed his foot on the back of the dog's head and pressed. The dog snarled and bit him on the ankle. We moved on.

The *stade* was recovering from lunch, the small folding tables under the trees still scattered with scraps of food and empty glasses. A spaniel had managed to jump on to one of the tables and clear it up, and was asleep with its chin in a plate. Spectators moved with the slowness that comes from a full belly and a hot day, picking their teeth as they inspected the offerings of the local arms dealer.

On a long trestle table, thirty or forty guns were laid

neatly in a row, including the new sensation that was attracting great interest. It was a matt black pump-action riot gun. If there were ever to be a mass uprising of bloodthirsty killer rabbits in the forest, this was undoubtedly the machine one needed to keep them in order. But some of the other items puzzled us. What would a hunter do with brass knuckle-dusters and sharpened steel throwing stars, as used, so a hand-printed card said, by the Japanese Ninja? It was a selection that contrasted violently with the rubber bones and squeaky toys on sale at English dog shows.

It is always possible, when dogs and owners gather together *en masse*, to find living proof of the theory that they grow to resemble each other. In other parts of the world, this may be confined to physical characteristics – ladies and basset hounds with matching jowls, whiskery little men with bushy eyebrows and scotties, emaciated ex-jockeys with their whippets. But, France being France, there seems to be a deliberate effort to emphasize the resemblance through fashion, by choosing *ensembles* that turn dog and owner into co-ordinated accessories.

There were two clear winners in the Ménerbes *Concours d'Élégance*, perfectly complementary and visibly very pleased with the attention they were attracting from less modish spectators. In the ladies' section, a blonde with white shirt, white shorts, white cowboy boots and white miniature poodle on a white lead picked her way fastidiously through the dust to sip, with little finger cocked, an Orangina at the bar. The ladies of the village, sensibly dressed in skirts and flat shoes, looked at her with the same critical interest they usually reserve for cuts of meat in the butcher's.

The male entries were dominated by a thickset man with a waist-high Great Dane. The dog was pure, shiny black.

The man wore a tight black T-shirt, even tighter black jeans and black cowboy boots. The dog wore a heavy chain-link collar. The man wore a necklace like a small hawser, with a medallion that thudded against his sternum with every step, and a similarly important bracelet. By some oversight, the dog wasn't wearing a bracelet, but they made a virile pair as they posed on the high ground. The man gave the impression of having to control his massive beast by brute force, yanking on the collar and growling. The dog, as placid as Great Danes normally are, had no idea he was supposed to be vicious or restive, and observed smaller dogs passing underneath him with polite interest.

We were wondering how long the Great Dane's good humour would last before he ate one of the tiny dogs that clustered like flies round his back legs when we were ambushed by Monsieur Mathieu and his tombola tickets. For a mere 10 francs, he was offering us a chance to win one of the sporting and gastronomic treasures donated by local tradesmen: a mountain bike, a microwave oven, a shotgun or a *maxi saucisson*. I was relieved that puppies weren't among the prizes. Monsieur Mathieu leered. 'You never know what might be in the *saucisson*,' he said. And then, seeing the horror on my wife's face, he patted her. '*Non, non. Je rigole.*'

In fact, there were enough puppies on display to make a mountain of *saucissons*. They lay or squirmed in piles under almost every tree, on blankets, in cardboard cartons, in homemade kennels and on old sweaters. It was a testing time as we went from one furry, multi-legged heap to the next. My wife is highly susceptible to anything with four feet and a wet nose, and the sales tactics of the owners were shameless. At the slightest sign of interest, they would pluck a puppy from the pile and thrust it into her arms, where it would promptly go to sleep. '*Voilà! Comme il est content!*' I could see her weakening by the minute.

We were saved by the loudspeaker introducing the expert who was to give the commentary on the field trials. He was in *tenue de chasse* – khaki cap, shirt and trousers – with a deep tobacco voice. He was unused to speaking into a microphone and, being Provençal, he was unable to keep his hands still. Thus his explanation came and went in intermittent snatches as he pointed the microphone helpfully at various parts of the field while his words disappeared into the breeze.

The competitors were lined up at the far end, half a dozen pointers and two mud-coloured dogs of impenetrable ancestry. Small clumps of brushwood had been placed at random around the field. These were the *bosquets* in which the game – a live quail which was held aloft by the quail-handler for inspection – was to be hidden.

The *chasseur*'s microphone technique improved enough for us to hear him explain that the quail would be tethered in a different *bosquet* for each competitor, and that it would not be killed (unless it was scared to death) by the dogs. They would simply indicate its hiding place, and the fastest find would win.

The quail was hidden, and the first competitor unleashed. He passed by two clumps with barely a sniff and then, still yards away from the third, stiffened and stopped.

'*Aha! Il est fort, ce chien,*' boomed the *chasseur*. The dog looked up for a second, distracted by the noise, before continuing his approach. He was now walking in slow motion, placing one paw on the ground with exaggerated care before lifting another, his neck and head stretched towards the *bosquet*, unwavering despite the *chasseur*'s admiring comments about his concentration and the delicacy of his movements.

Three feet away from the petrified quail, the dog froze, one front paw raised, with head, neck, back and tail in a perfect straight line.

'*Tiens! Bravo!*' said the *chasseur*, and started to clap, forgetting that he had a microphone in one hand. The owner retrieved his dog, and the two of them returned to the starting point in a triumphant competition trot. The official timekeeper, a lady in high heels and an elaborate black and white dress with flying panels, marked the dog's performance on a clipboard. The quail-handler dashed out to replant the quail in another *bosquet*, and the second contestant was sent on his way.

He went immediately to the *bosquet* recently vacated by the quail, and stopped.

'*Beh oui*,' said the *chasseur*, 'the scent is still strong there. But wait.' We waited. The dog waited. Then he got tired of waiting, and possibly annoyed at being sent out on a fool's errand. He lifted his leg on the *bosquet* and went back to his owner.

The quail-handler moved the unfortunate quail to a new hiding place, but it must have been a particularly pungent bird, because dog after dog stopped at one or other of the empty clumps, head cocked and paw tentatively raised, before giving up. An old man standing next to us explained the problem. The quail, he said, should have been walked on its lead from one *bosquet* to the next so that it left a scent. How else could a dog be expected to find him? Dogs are not *clairvoyants*. The old man shook his head and made soft clicking noises of disapproval with his tongue against his teeth.

The final competitor, one of the mud-coloured dogs, had been showing signs of increasing excitement as he watched the others being sent off, whining with impatience and tugging at his lead. When his turn came, it was obvious that he misunderstood the rules of the competition. Disregarding the quail and the *bosquets*, he completed the circuit of the *stade* at full speed before racing into the vines, followed by his bellowing owner. '*Oh là là*,' said the *chasseur*. '*Une locomotive. Tant pis.*'

Later, as the sun dipped and the shadows grew longer, Monsieur Dufour, president of '*Le Philosophe*' hunting club, presented the prizes before settling down with his colleagues to a gigantic paella. Long after dark, we could hear the distant sounds of laughter and clinking glasses and, some-where in the vines, the man shouting for his mud-coloured dog.

11

As Advertised in Vogue

Perhaps because he still has memories of his earlier life as a homeless, hungry stray, Boy takes every opportunity to make himself as agreeable as possible around the house. He brings gifts – a fallen bird's nest, a vine root, a half-masticated espadrille that he has been saving, a mouthful of undergrowth from the forest – and deposits them under the dining table with a messy generosity that he obviously feels will endear him to us. He contributes to the housework by leaving trails of leaves and dusty paw-prints on the floor. He assists in the kitchen, acting as a mobile receptacle for any scraps that may fall from above. He is never more than a few feet away, desperately, noisily, clumsily anxious to please.

His efforts to charm are not confined exclusively to us, and he has his own unorthodox but well-meaning style of greeting visitors to the house. Dropping the tennis ball that he normally keeps tucked in one side of his enormous mouth, he buries his equally enormous head in the groin of anyone who comes through the door. It's his version of a manly handshake, and our friends have come to expect it. They carry on talking, and Boy, his social duties done, retires to collapse on the nearest pair of feet.

The reactions to his welcome reflect, with some accuracy, the change of the seasons. During the winter, when our visitors, like us, are people who live in the Lubéron throughout the year, the head in the groin is either ignored or patted, leaves and twigs are brushed off old corduroy trousers, and the smooth progress of glass to mouth continues without interruption. When this is replaced by starts of surprise, spilt drinks and flustered attempts to fend off the questing snout from clean white clothes, we know that summer has arrived. And with it, the summer people.

Each year, there are more of them, coming down for the sun and the scenery as they always have, and now encouraged by two more recent attractions.

The first is practical: Provence is becoming more accessible every year. There is talk of the TGV high-speed train from Paris cutting half an hour off its already quick four-hour service to Avignon. The tiny airport just outside the town is being extended, and will undoubtedly soon be calling itself Avignon International. A giant green model of the Statue of Liberty has been erected in front of Marseille airport to announce direct flights twice a week to and from New York.

At the same time, Provence has been 'discovered' yet again – and not only Provence in general, but the towns and villages where we shop for food and rummage through the markets. Fashion has descended upon us.

The bible of the Beautiful People, *Women's Wear Daily*, which pronounces on the proper length of hem, size of bust and weight of earrings in New York, ventured last year into St Rémy and the Lubéron. High-profile summer residents were shown squeezing their aubergines, sipping their *kirs*, admiring their barbered cypress trees and generally getting away from it all – with each other and an attendant photographer, *bien sûr* – to revel in the pleasures of the simple country life.

In American *Vogue*, the world's most cloyingly pungent magazine with its impregnated perfume advertisements, an article on the Lubéron was sandwiched between Athena Starwoman's horoscopes and a Paris Bistro Update. In the introduction to the article, the Lubéron was described as 'the secret South of France' – a secret that lasted two lines before it was also described as the country's most fashionable area. How the two go together is a contradiction that only a plausible sub-editor could explain.

The editors of French *Vogue*, of course, were in on the secret as well. Indeed, they had known about it for some time, as they made clear to the reader in the introduction to their article. In fine world-weary vein, they led off by saying *le Lubéron, c'est fini*, followed by some disparaging suggestions that it might be snobbish, expensive and altogether *démodé*.

Could they really have meant it? No, they couldn't. Far from being finished, the Lubéron is apparently still attracting Parisians and foreigners who, according to *Vogue*, are *often famous*. (How often? Once a week? Twice a week? They didn't say.) And then we are invited to meet them. Come with us, *Vogue* says, into their very private world.

Goodbye privacy. For the next twelve pages, we are treated to photographs of the often famous with their children, their dogs, their gardens, their friends and their swimming pools. There is a map – *le who's who* – showing where the chic members of Lubéron society are trying, rather unsuccessfully it seems, to hide themselves. But hiding is out of the question. These poor devils can't even have a swim or a drink without a photographer darting out of the bushes to capture the moment for the delectation of *Vogue*'s readers.

Among the photographs of artists, writers, decorators, politicians and tycoons is a picture of a man who, as the caption says, knows all the houses in the area and who accepts three dinner invitations at the same time. The reader may think that this is merely the result of a deprived childhood or an insatiable craving for *gigot en croûte*, but it is nothing of the kind. Our man is working. He is a real estate agent. He needs to know who's looking, who's buying and who's selling, and there just aren't enough dinners in the normal day to keep him *au courant*.

It's a hectic business being a real estate agent in the Lubéron, particularly now that the area is passing through a fashionable phase. Property prices have inflated like a three-dinner stomach, and even during our short time as residents, we have seen increases that defy reason or belief. A pleasant old ruin with half a roof and a few acres of land was offered to some friends for 3 million francs. Other friends decided to build instead of converting, and were in shock for a week at the estimate: 5 million francs. A house with possibilities in one of the favoured villages? One million francs.

Naturally, the agent's fees are geared to these zero-encrusted prices, although the exact percentage varies. We have heard of commissions ranging from 3 to 8 per cent, sometimes paid by the seller, sometimes by the buyer.

It can add up to a very comfortable living. And, to the outsider, it may appear to be a congenial way to earn that living; it's always interesting to look at houses, and often the buyers and sellers are interesting as well (not always honest or reliable, as we shall see, but seldom dull). As a *métier*, being a property agent in a desirable part of the world theoretically offers a stimulating and lucrative way to pass the time in between dinners.

It is not, alas, without its problems, and the first of these is competition. Nearly six yellow pages in the Vaucluse telephone directory are taken up by real estate agents and their advertisements – properties of style, properties of character, exclusive properties, quality properties, hand-picked properties, properties of guaranteed charm – the house-hunter is spoiled for choice and baffled by the terminology. What is the difference between character and style? Should one go for something exclusive or something hand-picked? The only way to find out is to take your dreams and your budget along to an agent and spend a morning, a day, a week among the *bastides*, the *mas*, the *maisons de charme* and the white elephants that are currently on offer.

Finding an agent in the Lubéron is no more difficult than finding a butcher. In the old days, the village *notaire* used to be the man who knew if *Mère* Bertrand was selling off her old farm, or if a recent death had made a house empty and available. To a large extent, the *notaire*'s function as a property scout has been taken over by the agent, and almost every village has one. Ménerbes has two. Bonnieux has three. The more fashionable Gordes had, at the last count, four. (It was in Gordes that we saw competition in the raw. One agent was distributing flyers to all the cars parked in the Place du Château. He was followed at a discreet distance by a second agent who was taking the flyers off the windscreens and replacing them with his own. Unfortunately, we had to leave before seeing if the third and fourth agents were lurking behind a buttress waiting for their turn.)

Without exception, these agents are initially charming and helpful, and they have dossiers filled with photographs of ravishing properties, some of them actually priced at less than seven figures. These, inevitably, are the ones that have just been sold, but there are others – mills, nunneries, shepherds' hovels, grandiose *maisons de maître*, turreted follies and farmhouses of every shape and size. What a selection! And this is only one agent.

But if you should go to see a second agent, or a third, you may experience a definite feeling of *déjà vu*. There is something familiar about many of the properties. The photographs have been taken from different angles, but there's no doubt about it. These are the same mills and nunneries and farmhouses that you saw in the previous dossier. And there you have the second problem which bedevils the life of a Lubéron agent: there are not enough properties to go round.

Building restrictions in most parts of the Lubéron are fairly stringent, and they are more or less observed by everyone except farmers, who seem to be able to build at will. And so the supply of what agents would call properties with *beaucoup d'allure* is limited. This situation brings out the hunting instinct, and many agents during the less busy winter months will spend days driving around, eyes and ears open for signs or rumour that an undiscovered jewel may shortly be coming on the market. If it is, and if the agent is quick and persuasive enough, there is the chance of an exclusive arrangement and full commission. What usually happens, though, is that a seller will retain two or three agents and leave them to sort out the delicate matter of how the fees should be split.

More problems. Who introduced the client? Who showed the property first? The agents may be obliged to collaborate, but the competitive streak is barely hidden, and nothing brings it out in the open faster than a little misunderstanding about the division of the spoils. Accusations and counter-accusations, heated phone calls, pointed remarks about unethical behaviour – even, as a last resort, an appeal to the client to act as referee – all these unhappy complications have been known to upset liaisons that started off with such high hopes. That is why the *cher collègue* of yesterday can turn into the *escroc* of today. *C'est dommage, mais . . .*

There are other, heavier crosses for the agent to bear, and these are the clients, with their unpredictable and frequently shady behaviour. What is it that turns the outwardly trust-worthy and respectable minnow into a shark? Money has a lot to do with it, obviously, but there is also a determination to do a deal, to haggle up to the last minute and down to the final light bulb, which is not so much a matter of francs and centimes as a desire to win, to out-negotiate the other side. And the agent is stuck in the middle.

The tussle over the price is probably the same throughout the world, but in the Lubéron there is an added local complication to muddy the waters of negotiation still further. More often than not, prospective buyers are Parisians or foreigners, while prospective sellers are *paysans du coin*. There is a considerable difference between the attitude that each side brings to business dealings which can cause everyone con-cerned in the transaction weeks or months of exasperation.

The peasant finds it hard to take yes for an answer. If the price he has asked for his grandmother's old *mas* is agreed without any quibbling, he has an awful suspicion that he has underpriced the property. This would cause him grief for the rest of his days, and his wife would nag him endlessly about the better price that a neighbour obtained for *his* grand-mother's old *mas*. And so, just when the buyers think they have bought, the seller is having second thoughts. Adjust-ments will have to be made. The peasant arranges a rendez-vous with the agent to clarify certain details.

He tells the agent that he may have neglected to say that a field adjoining the house – the very same field, as luck would have it, with the well in the corner and a good supply of water – is not included in the price. *Pas grand' chose*, but he thought he'd better mention it.

Consternation from the buyers. The field was *undoubtedly* included in the price. In fact, it is the only possible place on the property flat enough for the tennis court. Their dismay is communicated to the peasant, who shrugs. What does he care about tennis courts? Nevertheless, he is a reasonable man. It is a fertile and valuable field, and he would hate to part with such a treasure, but he might be prepared to listen to an offer.

Buyers are usually impatient, and short of time. They work in Paris or Zürich or London, and they can't be coming down to the Lubéron every five minutes to look at houses. The peasant, on the other hand, is never in a hurry. He's not going anywhere. If the property doesn't sell this year, he'll put up the price and sell it next year.

Back and forth the discussions go, with the agent and the buyers becoming increasingly irritated. But when a deal is eventually done, as it usually is, the new owners try to put all thoughts of resentment behind them. It is, after all, a wonderful property, a *maison de rêve*, and to celebrate the purchase they decide to take a picnic and spend the day wandering through the rooms and planning the changes they're going to make.

Something, however, is not as it should be. The handsome old cast-iron bathtub with the claw feet has disappeared from the bathroom. The buyers call the agent. The agent calls the peasant. Where is the bathtub?

The bathtub? His sainted grandmother's bathtub? The

bathtub that is a family heirloom? Surely nobody would expect a rare object of such sentimental value to be included in the sale of a house? Nevertheless, he is a reasonable man, and might possibly be persuaded to consider an offer.

It is incidents such as this that have led buyers to tread warily along the path that leads to the *acte de vente* when the house will officially be theirs – sometimes behaving with the caution of a lawyer approaching an opinion. Inventories are made of shutters and door-knockers and kitchen sinks, of logs in the woodstore and tiles on the floor and trees in the garden. And in one marvellously mistrustful episode, even multiple inventories were thought to be insufficient protection against last-minute chicanery.

Fearing the worst, the buyer had engaged a local *huissier*, or commissioner for oaths. His task was to verify, beyond any shadow of legal doubt, that the seller was leaving behind the lavatory paper holders. It is tempting to imagine the two of them, seller and *huissier*, jammed together in the confined space of the lavatory to conduct the formalities: 'Raise your right hand and repeat after me: I solemnly swear to leave intact and functioning these fittings hereafter described . . .' The mind boggles.

Despite these and a hundred other snags, properties continue to sell at prices that would have been inconceivable ten years ago. I recently heard Provence being enthusiastically promoted by an agent as 'the California of Europe', not only because of the climate, but also because of something indefinable and yet irresistible which was originally invented in California: the Lifestyle.

As far as I can make out, the Lifestyle is achieved by transforming a rural community into a kind of sophisticated holiday camp, with as many urban conveniences as possible and, if there's any spare land, a golf course. If this had been going on in our corner of Provence, I had missed it, and so I asked the agent where I should go to see what he was talking about. Where was the nearest Lifestyle centre?

He looked at me as though I'd been hiding in a time warp. 'Haven't you been to Gordes recently?' he said.

We first saw Gordes sixteen years ago, and in a region of beautiful villages it was the most spectacularly beautiful of all. Honey-coloured and perched on the top of a hill, with long views across the plain to the Lubéron, it was what estate agents would call a gem, a picture postcard come to life. There was a Renaissance château, narrow streets cobbled in rectangular stone and the modest facilities of an unspoiled village: a butcher, two bakers, a simple hotel, a seedy café and a post office run by a man recruited, we were sure, for his unfailing surliness.

The countryside behind the village, permanently green with its covering of scrub oak and pine, was patterned with narrow paths bordered by dry stone walls. You could walk for hours without being aware of any houses except for the rare glimpse of an old tiled roof among the trees. We were told that building was so restricted as to be virtually forbidden.

That was sixteen years ago. Today, Gordes is still beautiful – from a distance, at any rate. But as you reach the bottom of the road that leads up to the village, you are greeted by a ladder of signs, each rung advertising an hotel, a restaurant, a *salon de thé* – every comfort and attraction for the visitor is labelled except the *toilettes publiques*.

At regular intervals along the road are reproduction nineteenth-century street lamps which look spiky and incongruous against the weathered stone walls and houses. On the bend where the village comes into view, at least one car has always stopped to allow driver and passengers to take photographs. On the final bend before the village, a large area of tarmac has been laid down for car parking. If you choose to ignore this and drive up into the village, you will probably have to come back. The Place du Château, now also coated in tarmac, is usually fully booked with cars from all over Europe.

The old hotel is still there, but it has a new hotel as its next door neighbour. A few metres further on, there is a sign for Sidney Food, *Spécialiste Modules Fast-Food*. Then there is a Souleiado boutique. Then the once-seedy café, now spruced up. In fact, everything has been spruced up, the curmudgeon in the post office has been retired, the *toilettes publiques* enlarged and the village turned into a place for visitors rather than inhabitants. Official Gordes T-shirts can be bought to prove you've been there.

A kilometre or so up the road is another hotel, walled off from public view and equipped with a helicopter landing pad. The building restrictions in the *garrigue* have been relaxed and an enormous sign, subtitled in English, advertises luxury villas with electronic security entrance and fully fitted bathrooms at prices from 2,500,000 francs.

So far, there are no signs to indicate where *Vogue*'s often famous people have their country homes, so passengers in the procession of huge coaches on their way to the twelfth-century Abbaye de Sénanque are left to speculate whose half-hidden house they're looking at. One day, someone of enterprise and vision will produce a map similar to those Hollywood guides to the houses of the stars, and then we shall feel even closer to California. Meanwhile, jacuzzis and joggers are no longer sufficiently exotic to attract any attention, and the hills are alive with the thwack of tennis balls and the drowsy hum of the cement-mixer.

It has often happened before, in many other parts of the world. People are attracted to an area because of its beauty and its promise of peace, and then they transform it into a high-rent suburb complete with cocktail parties, burglar alarm systems, four-wheel-drive recreational vehicles and other essential trappings of *la vie rustique*.

I don't think the locals mind. Why should they? Barren patches of land that couldn't support a herd of goats are suddenly worth millions of francs. Shops and restaurants and hotels prosper. The *maçons*, the carpenters, the landscape gardeners and the tennis court builders have bulging order books, and everyone benefits from *le boum*. Cultivating tourists is much more rewarding than growing grapes.

It hasn't yet affected Ménerbes too much; not, at least, in an obviously visible way. The *Café du Progrès* is still resolutely unchic. The small, smart restaurant that opened two years ago has closed, and apart from a small, smart estate agent's office, the centre of the village looks much the same as it did when we first saw it several years ago.

But change is in the air. Ménerbes has been awarded a sign, *Un des plus beaux villages de France*, and some of the inhabitants seem to have developed a sudden awareness of the media.

My wife came across three venerable ladies sitting in a row on a stone wall, their three dogs sitting in a row in front of them. It made a nice picture, and my wife asked if she could take a photograph.

The senior old lady looked at her and thought for a moment. 'What's it for?' she said. Obviously, *Vogue* had been there first.

12

Mainly Dry Periods,
with Scattered Fires

Like some of our agricultural neighbours in the valley, we
subscribe to a service provided by the meteorological station
at Carpentras. Twice a week, we receive detailed weather
forecasts on mimeographed sheets. They predict, usually
very accurately, our ration of sun and rain, the likelihood of
storms and Mistral and the temperature ranges throughout
the Vaucluse.

As the early weeks of 1989 went by, the forecasts and
statistics began to show ominous signs that the weather was
not behaving as it should. There was not enough rain; not
nearly enough.

The previous winter had been mild, with so little snow in
the mountains that the torrents of spring would be no more
than dribbles. Winter had also been dry. January's rainfall
was 9.5 millimetres; normally it is just over 60 millimetres.
February's rainfall was down. The same in March. Summer
fire regulations – no burning in the fields – were put into
effect early. The traditionally wet Vaucluse spring was only
moist, and early summer wasn't even moist. Cavaillon's May
rainfall was 1 millimetre, compared with the average 54.6;
7 millimetres in June, compared with the average 44. Wells

were going dry, and there was a significant drop in the water level of the Fontaine de Vaucluse.

Drought in the Lubéron hangs over the farmers like an overdue debt. Conversations in the fields and in the village streets are gloomy as the crops bake and the earth turns brittle and crusty. And there is always the risk of fire, terrible to think about but impossible to forget.

All it takes is a spark in the forest – a carelessly dropped cigarette end, a smouldering match – and the Mistral will do the rest, turning a flicker into a fire, and then into an explosion of flame that rips through the trees faster than a running man. We had heard about a young *pompier* who died in the spring, near Murs. He had been facing the flames when a flying spark, maybe from a pine cone that had burst into red-hot fragments, had landed in the trees behind him, cutting him off. It had happened in seconds.

That is tragic enough when the cause of the fire is accidental, but sickening when it is deliberate. Sadly, it often is. Droughts attract pyromaniacs, and they could hardly have asked for better conditions than the summer of 1989. One man had been caught in the spring setting fire to the *garrigue*. He was young, and he wanted to be a *pompier*, but the fire service had turned him down. He was taking his revenge with a box of matches.

Our first sight of smoke was on the hot, windy evening of the 14th of July. Overhead was cloudless, the clean, burnished blue sky that the Mistral often brings, and it accentuated the black stain that was spreading above Roussillon, a few miles away across the valley. As we watched it from the path above the house, we heard the drone of engines, and a formation of Canadair planes flew low over the Lubéron, ponderous with their cargoes of water. Then helicopters, the *bombardiers d'eau*. From Bonnieux came the insistent, panicky blare of a fire siren, and we both looked nervously behind us. Less than 100 yards separates our house from the tree-line, and 100 yards is nothing to a well-stoked fire with a gale force wind at its back.

That evening, as the Canadairs, heavy-bellied and slow, ferried between the fire and the sea, we had to face the possibility that the next stretch of forest to go up in flames might be closer to home. The *pompiers* who had come with their calendars at Christmas had told us what we were supposed to do: cut off the electricity, close the wooden shutters, hose them down, stay in the house. We had joked about taking refuge in the wine cellar with a couple of glasses and a corkscrew – better to be roasted drunk than sober. It no longer seemed funny.

The wind dropped as night came, and the glow over Roussillon might have been no more than floodlights on the village *boules* court. We checked on the weather forecast before going to bed. It was not good: *beau temps très chaud et ensoleillé, Mistral fort.*

The next day's copy of *Le Provençal* carried details of the Roussillon fire. It had destroyed more than 100 acres of the pine woods around the village before 400 *pompiers*, ten aircraft and the *soldats du feu* from the army had put it out. There were photographs of horses and a herd of goats being led to safety, and of a solitary *pompier* silhouetted against a wall of flame. Three smaller fires were reported in the same article. It would probably have made the front page except for the arrival of the Tour de France in Marseille.

We drove across to Roussillon a few days later. What had been pine-green and beautiful was now desolate – charred, ugly tree-stumps jutting like rotten teeth from the ochre-red

earth of the hillsides. Miraculously, some of the houses seemed untouched despite the devastation that surrounded them. We wondered if the owners had stayed inside or run, and tried to imagine what it must have been like to sit in a dark house listening to the fire coming closer and closer, feeling its heat through the walls.

July's rainfall was 5 millimetres, but the wise men of the café told us that the storms of August would soak the Lubéron and allow the *pompiers* to relax. Always, we were told, *le quinze août* brought a downpour, swilling campers out of their tents, flooding roads, drenching the forest and, with luck, drowning the pyromaniacs.

Day after day we looked for rain, and day after day we saw nothing but sun. Lavender that we had planted in the spring died. The patch of grass in front of the house abandoned its ambitions to become a lawn and turned the dirty yellow of poor straw. The earth shrank, revealing its knuckles and bones, rocks and roots that had been invisible before. The luckier peasants who had powerful irrigation systems began to water their vines. Our vines drooped. Faustin, on his tours of inspection in the vineyard, drooped also.

The pool was as warm as soup, but at least it was wet, and one evening the scent of water attracted a tribe of *sangliers*. Eleven of them came out of the forest and stopped fifty yards from the house. One boar took advantage of the halt and mounted his mate, and Boy, showing uncharacteristic bravado, went dancing towards the happy couple, his bark soprano with excitement. Still joined together like competitors in a wheelbarrow race, they chased him off, and he returned to the door of the courtyard where he could be noisy and brave in safety. The *sangliers* changed their minds about the pool, and filed away through the vines to eat Jacky's melons in the field on the other side of the road.

Le quinze août was as dry as the first half of the month had been, and every time the Mistral blew we waited for the sound of the sirens and the Canadairs. A pyromaniac had actually telephoned the *pompiers*, promising another fire as soon as there was enough wind, and there were daily helicopter patrols over the valley.

But they didn't see him when he did it again, this time near Cabrières. Ashes carried by the wind fell in the courtyard, and the sun was blotted out by smoke. The smell of it spooked the dogs, who paced and whined and barked at gusts of wind. The red and pink evening sky was hidden behind a smear of grey, faintly luminous, sombre and frightening.

A friend who was staying in Cabrières came over to see us that night. Some houses on the edge of the village had been evacuated. She had brought her passport with her, and a spare pair of knickers.

We saw no fires after that, although the pyromaniac had made more phone calls, always threatening the Lubéron. August ended. The rainfall reported for our area was 0.0, compared with the average of 52. When a half-hearted shower came in September, we stood out in it and took great breaths of cool, damp air. For the first time in weeks, the forest smelt fresh.

With the immediate danger of fire behind them, the local inhabitants felt sufficiently relieved to complain about the effects of the drought on their stomachs. With the exception of the year's wine, which in Châteauneuf was announced as spectacularly good, the gastronomic news was disastrous. The lack of rain in July would mean a miserable truffle crop in the winter, few in number and small in size. Hunters would have to shoot each other for sport; game that had left the parched Lubéron to look for water further north was unlikely to come back. Autumn at the table would not be the same, *pas du tout normal*.

Our education suffered. Monsieur Menicucci, whose many talents included an ability to detect and identify the wild mushrooms in the forest, had promised to take us on an expedition – kilos of mushrooms, he said, would be there for the taking. He would instruct us, and supervise afterwards in the kitchen, assisted by a bottle of Cairanne.

But October came and the hunt had to be cancelled. For the first time in Menicucci's memory, the forest was bare. He came to the house one morning, knife, stick and basket at the ready, snakeproof boots tightly laced, and spent a fruitless hour poking among the trees before giving up. We would have to try again next year. Madame his wife would be disappointed, and so would his friend's cat, who was a great *amateur* of wild mushrooms.

A cat?

Beh oui, but a cat with an extraordinary nose, able to pick out dangerous or deadly mushrooms. Nature is mysterious and wonderful, said Menicucci, and often cannot be explained in a scientific manner.

I asked what the cat did with edible mushrooms. He eats them, said Menicucci, but not raw. They must be cooked in olive oil and sprinkled with chopped parsley. That is his little weakness. *C'est bizarre, non?*

The forest was officially recognized as a tinder-box in November, when it was invaded by the *Office National des Forêts*. One dark, overcast morning I was about two miles from the house when I saw a billow of smoke and heard the rasp of brushcutters. In a clearing at the end of the track, army trucks were parked next to an enormous yellow machine, perhaps ten feet high, a cross between a bulldozer and a mammoth tractor. Men in olive-drab fatigue uniforms moved through the trees, sinister in their goggles and helmets, hacking away the undergrowth and throwing it on the fire that hissed with sizzling sap from the green wood.

An officer, hard-faced and lean, looked at me as though I was trespassing and barely nodded when I said *bonjour*. A bloody civilian, and a foreigner as well.

I turned to go home, and stopped to look at the yellow monster. The driver, a fellow civilian from the look of his cracked leather waistcoat and non-regulation checked cap, was cursing as he tried to loosen a tight nut. He exchanged his spanner for a mallet – the all-purpose Provençal remedy for obstinate mechanical equipment – which made me sure he wasn't an army man. I tried another *bonjour*, and this time it was more amiably received.

He could have been Santa Claus's younger brother; without the beard, but with ruddy round cheeks and bright eyes and a moustache that was flecked with the sawdust that was blowing in the wind. He waved his mallet in the direction of the extermination squad in the trees. '*C'est comme la guerre, eh?*'

He called it, in correct military style, *opération débroussaillage*. Twenty metres on either side of the track that led towards Ménerbes were to be cleared of undergrowth and thinned out to reduce the risk of fire. His job was to follow the men in his machine and shred everything they hadn't burned. He banged its yellow side with the flat of his hand. 'This will eat a tree trunk and spit it out as twigs.'

It took the men a week to cover the distance to the house. They left the edge of the forest shorn, the clearings smudged with pools of ashes. And following on, chewing and spitting a few hundred metres each day, came the yellow monster with its relentless, grinding appetite.

The driver came down to see us one evening, asking for a glass of water, easily persuaded into a glass of *pastis*. He apologized for parking at the top of the garden. Parking was a daily problem, he said; with a top speed of ten kilometres an hour he could hardly take what he described as his little toy back home to Apt each night.

He took off his cap for the second glass of *pastis*. It was good to have someone to talk to, he said, after a day on his own with nothing to listen to but the racket of his machine. But it was necessary work. The forest had been left untended too long. It was choked with dead wood, and if there was another drought next year . . . *pof!*

We asked him if the pyromaniac had ever been caught, and he shook his head. The madman with the *briquet*, he called him. Let's hope he spends his holidays in the Cévennes next year.

The driver of the yellow monster came again the following evening and brought us a Camembert, which he told us how to cook – the way he did when he was in the forest during the winter and needed something to keep out the cold.

'You make a fire,' he said, arranging imaginary branches on the table in front of him, 'and you take the cheese from the box and remove the paper wrapping. And then you put it back, *d'accord?*' To make sure we had understood, he held up the Camembert and tapped its thin wooden box.

'*Bon*. Now you put the box in the embers of the fire. The box burns. The rind of the cheese turns black. The cheese

melts, but . . .' an instructive finger was raised for emphasis
'. . . he is sealed inside the rind. He cannot escape into the
fire.'

A swig of *pastis*, the moustache wiped with the back of the
hand.

'*Alors*, you take your *baguette* and split it all the way down.
Now – *attention aux doigts* – you take the cheese from the fire,
you make a hole in the rind, and you pour the melted cheese
into the bread. *Et voilà!*'

He grinned, his red cheeks bunching under his eyes, and
patted his stomach. Sooner or later, as we now expected, every
conversation in Provence seems to turn to food or drink.

At the beginning of 1990, we were sent the weather statistics
for the previous year. Despite an unusually wet November,
our annual rainfall was less than half the normal amount.

There has been another mild winter. The water levels are still
below what they should be, and it is estimated that as much as
30 per cent of the undergrowth in the forest is dead, and
therefore dry. The first big fire of summer destroyed more than
6,000 acres near Marseille, cutting off the *autoroute* in two places.
And the madman with the *briquet* is still at large; probably, like
us, taking a keen interest in the weather forecasts.

We have bought a heavy-gauge tin box to hold all those
pieces of paper – passports, *attestations*, birth certificates,
contrats, *permis*, old electricity bills – that are essential in
France to prove your existence. To lose the house in a fire
would be a disaster, but to lose our identities at the same
time would make life impossible. The tin box is going in the
farthest corner of the *cave*, next to the Châteauneuf.

Every time it rains we're delighted, which Faustin takes
as a promising sign that we are becoming less English.

13

No Spitting in Châteauneuf-du-Pape

August in Provence is a time to lie low, to seek shade, to move slowly and to limit your excursions to very short distances. Lizards know best, and I should have known better.

It was in the high eighties by 9.30, and when I got into the car I immediately felt like a piece of chicken about to be *sautéed*. I looked at the map to find roads that would keep me away from the tourist traffic and heat-maddened truck drivers, and a bead of sweat dropped from my nose to score a direct hit on my destination – Châteauneuf-du-Pape, the small town with the big wine.

Months before, in the winter, I had met a man called Michel at a dinner to celebrate the engagement of two friends of ours. The first bottles of wine came. Toasts were proposed. But I noticed that while the rest of us were merely drinking, Michel was conducting a personal, very intense ritual.

He stared into his glass before picking it up, then cupped it in the palm of his hand and swirled it gently three or four times. Raising the glass to eye level, he peered at the traces of wine that his swirling had caused to trickle down the inner sides. His nose, with nostrils alert and flared, was presented to the wine and made a thorough investigation. Deep sniffing. One final swirl, and he took the first mouthful, but only on trial.

It obviously had to pass several tests before being allowed down the throat. Michel chewed it for a few reflective seconds. He pursed his lips and took a little air into his mouth and made discreet rinsing noises. Lifting his eyes to heaven, he flexed his cheeks in and out to encourage a free flow round tongue and molars and then, apparently satisfied with the wine's ability to withstand an oral assault course, he swallowed.

He noticed that I had been watching the performance, and grinned. '*Pas mal, pas mal.*' He took another, less elaborate swallow, and saluted the glass with raised eyebrows. 'It was a good year, '85.'

As I found out during dinner, Michel was a *négociant*, a professional wine drinker, a buyer of grapes and a seller of nectar. He specialized in the wines of the south, from Tavel *rosé* (the favourite wine, so he said, of Louis XIV) through the gold-tinged whites to the heavy, heady reds of Gigondas. But of all the wines in his extensive collection, his *merveille*, the one he would like to die drinking, was the Châteauneuf-du-Pape.

He described it as though he were talking about a woman. His hands caressed the air. Delicate kisses dusted his fingertips, and there was much talk of body and bouquet and *puissance*. It was not unknown, he said, for a Châteauneuf to reach fifteen degrees of alcoholic content. And these days, when Bordeaux seems to get thinner every year and the price of Burgundy is only possible for the Japanese, the wines of Châteauneuf are nothing less than bargains. I must come up to his *caves* and see for myself. He would arrange a *dégustation*.

The time that elapses in Provence between planning a rendezvous and keeping it can often stretch into months, and sometimes years, and so I wasn't expecting an immediate invitation. Winter turned to spring, spring turned to summer and summer melted into August, the most lethal month of the year to be toying with a fifteen-degree wine, and then Michel called.

'Tomorrow morning at eleven,' he said. 'In the *caves* at Châteauneuf. Eat plenty of bread at breakfast.'

I had done what he suggested and, as an extra precaution, taken a soup-spoonful of neat olive oil, which one of the local gourmets had told me was an excellent way to coat the stomach and cushion the system against repeated assault by young and powerful wines. In any case, I thought as I drove along the twisting, baked country roads, I wouldn't be swallowing much. I would do as the experts do, rinse and spit.

Châteauneuf came into view, trembling in the heat haze, just before eleven o'clock. It is a place entirely dedicated to wine. Seductive invitations are everywhere, on sunbleached peeling boards, on freshly painted posters, hand-lettered on monster bottles, fixed to the wall, propped at the side of vineyards, stuck on pillars at the end of driveways. *Dégustez! Dégustez!*

I drove through the gateway in the high stone wall that protects the Caves Bessac from the outside world, parked in the shade and unstuck myself from the car. I felt the sun come down on the top of my head like a close-fitting hat of hot air. In front of me was a long building, crenellated along the top, its façade blind except for huge double doors. A group of people, outlined against the black interior, were standing in the doorway, holding large bowls that glinted in the sun.

The *cave* felt almost cold, and the glass that Michel gave me was pleasantly cool in my hand. It was one of the biggest glasses I had ever seen, a crystal bucket on a stem, with a bulbous belly narrowing at the top to the circumference of a goldfish bowl. Michel said it could hold three-quarters of a bottle of wine.

My eyes adjusted to the gloom after the glare outside, and I began to realize that this was not a modest *cave*. Twenty-five thousand bottles would have been lost in the murk of one of the distant corners. In fact, there were no bottles to be seen, just boulevards of barrels – enormous barrels lying on their sides supported by waist-high platforms, their upper curves twelve or fifteen feet above the ground. Scrawled in chalk on the flat face of each barrel were descriptions of the contents, and for the first time in my life I was able to walk through a wine list: Côtes-du-Rhône-Villages, Lirac, Vac-queyras, Saint-Joseph, Crozes-Hermitage, Tavel, Gigondas – thousands of litres of each, arranged in vintages and dozing silently towards maturity.

'*Alors*,' said Michel, 'you can't walk around with an empty glass. What are you going to have?'

There was too much choice. I didn't know where to start. Would Michel guide me through the barrels? I could see that the others had something in their goldfish bowls; I'd have the same.

Michel nodded. That would be best, he said, because we only had two hours, and he didn't want to waste our time on the very young wines when there were so many treasures that were ready to drink. I was glad I'd had the olive oil.

Anything that qualified as a treasure was hardly spitting material. But two hours of swallowing would have me as supine as one of the barrels, and I asked if one was permitted to spit.

Michel waved his glass at a small drain that marked the entrance of the Boulevard Côtes-du-Rhône. '*Crachez si vous voulez, mais . . .*' It was clear that he thought it would be tragic to deny oneself the pleasure of the swallow, the bursting forth of flavours, the well-rounded finish and the profound satisfaction that comes from drinking a work of art.

The *maître de chai*, a wiry old man in a cotton jacket the colour of faded blue sky, appeared with a device that reminded me of a giant eye-dropper – three feet of glass tubing with a fist-sized rubber globe at one end. He aimed the nozzle and squeezed a generous measure of white wine into my glass, muttering a prayer as he squeezed: '*Hermitage '86, bouquet aux aromes de fleurs d'acacia. Sec, mais sans trop d'acidité.*'

I swirled and sniffed and rinsed and swallowed. Delicious. Michel was quite right. It would be a sin to consign this to the drain. With some relief, I saw that the others were tipping what they didn't drink into a large jug that stood on a nearby trestle table. Later, this would be transferred into a jar containing a *mère vinaigre*, and the result would be four-star vinegar.

Slowly, we worked our way down the boulevards. At each stop, the *maître de chai* climbed up his portable ladder to the top of the barrel, knocked out the bung and inserted his thirsty nozzle, returning down the ladder as carefully as if he were carrying a loaded weapon – which, as the tasting progressed, it began to resemble.

The first few shots had been confined to the whites, the

rosés and the lighter reds. But as we moved into the deeper gloom at the back of the *cave*, the wines too became darker. And heavier. And noticeably stronger. Each of them was served to the accompaniment of its own short but reverent litany. The red Hermitage, with its nose of violets, raspberries and mulberries, was a *vin viril*. The Côtes-du-Rhône *Grande Cuvée* was an elegant thoroughbred, fine and *étoffé*. I was impressed almost as much by the inventive vocabulary as by the wines themselves – fleshy, animal, muscular, well-built, voluptuous, sinewy – and the *maître* never repeated himself. I wondered whether he had been born with lyrical descriptive powers or whether he took a thesaurus to bed with him every night.

We finally arrived at Michel's *merveille*, the 1981 Châteauneuf-du-Pape. Although it would keep for many years to come, it was already a masterpiece, with its *robe profonde*, its hints of spice and truffle, its warmth, its balance – not to mention its alcoholic content, which was nudging fifteen degrees. I thought Michel was going to take a header into his glass. It's nice to see a man who loves his work.

With some reluctance, he put down his glass and looked at his watch. 'We must go,' he said. 'I'll get something to drink with lunch.' He went to an office at the front of the *cave*, and came out carrying a crate of a dozen bottles. He was followed by a colleague, carrying another dozen. Eight of us were going to lunch. How many would survive?

We left the *cave* and winced under the force of the sun. I had restrained myself to sips rather than mouthfuls; nevertheless, my head gave one sharp throb in warning as I walked to the car. Water. I must have water before even sniffing any more wine.

Michel thumped me on the back. 'There's nothing like a

dégustation to give you a thirst,' he said. 'Don't worry. We have a sufficiency.' Good grief.

The restaurant Michel had chosen was half an hour away, in the country outside Cavaillon. It was a *ferme auberge*, serving what he described as correct Provençal food in rustic surroundings. It was tucked away and hard to find, so I should stick closely to his car.

Easier said than done. So far as I know, there are no statistics to support my theory, but observation and heart-stopping personal experience have convinced me that a Frenchman with an empty stomach drives twice as fast as a Frenchman with a full stomach (which is already too fast for sanity and speed limits). And so it was with Michel. One minute he was there; the next he was a dust-smudged blur on the shimmering horizon, clipping the dry grass verges on the bends, booming through the narrow streets of villages in their midday coma, his gastronomic juices in overdrive. By the time we reached the restaurant, all pious thoughts of water were gone. I needed a drink.

The dining-room of the farm was cool and noisy. A large television set in the corner, ignored by the clientele, jabbered to itself. The other customers, mostly men, were darkened by the sun and dressed for outdoor work in old shirts and sleeveless vests, with the flattened hair and white foreheads that come from wearing a cap. A nondescript dog whiffled in the corner, nose twitching sleepily at the spicy smell of cooking meat coming from the kitchen. I realized that I was ravenous.

We were introduced to André, the *patron*, whose appearance, dark and full-bodied, fitted the description of some of the wines we'd been tasting. There were undertones of garlic, Gauloises and *pastis* present in his bouquet. He wore a loose shirt, short shorts, rubber sandals and an emphatic black moustache. He had a voice that transcended the hubbub of the room.

'*Eh, Michel! Qu'est-ce que c'est? Orangina? Coca-Cola?*' He started to unpack the crates of wine and reached in the back pocket of his shorts for a corkscrew. '*M'amour! Un seau, des glaçons, s'il te plaît.*'

His wife, sturdy and smiling, came out of the kitchen carrying a tray and unloaded it on the table: two ice buckets, plates of pink *saucisson* dotted with tiny peppercorns, a dish of vivid radishes and a deep bowl of thick *tapenade*, the olive and anchovy paste that is sometimes called the black butter of Provence. André was uncorking bottles like a machine, sniffing each cork as he drew it and arranging the bottles in a double line down the centre of the table. Michel explained that these were some of the wines we hadn't had time to try in the *cave*, young Côtes-du-Rhône for the most part, with half a dozen older and more serious reinforcements from Gigondas to help when the cheese arrived.

There is something about lunch in France that never fails to overcome any small reserves of will-power that I possess. I can sit down, resolved to be moderate, determined to eat and drink lightly, and be there three hours later, nursing my wine and still open to temptation. I don't think it's greed. I think it's the atmosphere generated by a roomful of people who are totally intent on eating and drinking. And while they do it, they talk about it; not about politics or sport or business, but about what is on the plate and in the glass. Sauces are compared, recipes argued over, past meals remembered and future meals planned. The world and its problems can be dealt with later on, but for the moment, *la bouffe* takes priority and contentment hangs in the air. I find it irresistible.

We eased into lunch like athletes limbering up. A radish, its top split open to hold a sliver of almost white butter and flecked with a pinch of coarse salt; a slice of *saucisson*, prickly with pepper on the tongue; rounds of toast made from yesterday's bread, shining with *tapenade*. Cool pink and white wines. Michel leaned across the table. 'No spitting.'

The *patron*, who was nipping away at a glass of red in between his duties, presented the first course with as much ceremony as a man in shorts and rubber sandals can muster, placing a deep *terrine*, its sides burnt almost black, on the table. He stuck an old kitchen knife into the *pâté*, then came back with a tall glass pot of *cornichons* and a dish of onion jam. '*Voilà, mes enfants. Bon appétit.*'

The wine changed colour as Michel dealt out his young reds, and the *terrine* was passed around the table for second slices. André came over from his card game to refill his glass. '*Ça va? Ça vous plaît?*' I told him how much I liked his onion jam. He told me to save some room for the next course, which was – he kissed his fingertips loudly – a triumph, *alouettes sans tête*, prepared specially for us by the hands of his adorable Monique.

Despite the rather grisly name (literally, larks without heads), it is a dish made from thin slices of beef rolled around slivers of salt pork, seasoned with chopped garlic and parsley, bathed in olive oil, dry white wine, stock and tomato *coulis* and served neatly trussed with kitchen twine. It looks nothing like a lark – more like an opulent sausage – but some creative Provençal cook must have thought that larks sounded more appetizing than rolled beef, and the name has survived.

Monique brought in the *alouettes*, which André said he had shot that morning. He was a man who found it difficult to make a joke without delivering the punch line physically, and the nudge he delivered with his forearm almost knocked me into a vast tub of *ratatouille*.

The headless larks were hot and humming with garlic, and Michel decided that they deserved a more solid wine. The Gigondas was promoted from the cheese course, and the collection of dead bottles at the end of the table was by now well into double figures. I asked Michel if he had any plans to work in the afternoon. He looked surprised. 'I *am* working,' he said. 'This is how I like to sell wine. Have another glass.'

Salad came, and then a basketwork tray of cheeses – fat white discs of fresh goat cheese, some mild Cantal and a wheel of creamy St Nectaire from the Auvergne. This inspired André, now installed at the head of the table, to produce another joke. There was this little boy in the Auvergne who was asked which he liked best, his mother or his father. The little boy thought for a moment. 'I like bacon best,' he said. André heaved with laughter. I was relieved to be out of nudging distance.

Scoops of sorbet were offered, and an apple tart, sleek with glaze, but I was defeated. When André saw me shake my head, he bellowed down the table, 'You must eat. You need your strength. We're going to have a game of *boules*.'

After coffee, he led us outside to show us the goats that he kept in a pen at the side of the restaurant. They were huddled in the shade of an outbuilding, and I envied them; they weren't being asked to play *boules* under a sun which was drilling lasers into the top of my head. It was no good. My eyes were aching from the glare and my stomach wanted desperately to lie down and digest in peace. I made my excuses, found a patch of grass under a plane tree and lowered my lunch to the ground.

André woke me some time after six and asked if I was staying for dinner. There were *pieds et paquets*, he said, and by some happy chance two or three bottles of the Gigondas had survived. With some difficulty, I escaped and drove home.

My wife had spent a sensible day in the shade and by the pool. She looked at me, a rumpled apparition, and asked if I had enjoyed myself.

'I hope they gave you something to eat,' she said.

14

Dinner with Pavarotti

The publicity preceded the event by months. Pictures of a
bearded face, crowned by a beret, appeared in newspapers
and on posters, and from spring onwards anyone in Provence
with half an ear for music had heard the news: Imperator
Pavarotti, as *Le Provençal* called him, was coming this summer
to sing for us. More than that, it would be the concert of a
lifetime, because of where he had chosen to perform. Not in
the Opera House in Avignon or the *salle de fêtes* in Gordes,
where he would be protected from the elements, but in the
open air, surrounded by ancient stones laid by his fellow
Italians nineteen centuries ago when they constructed the
Antique Theatre of Orange. Truly, *un événement éblouissant*.

Even empty, the Antique Theatre is overwhelming, a
place of colossal, almost unbelievable scale. It is in the form
of a D, and the straight wall which joins the two ends of the
semi-circle is 335 feet long, 120 feet high, and completely
intact. Apart from the patina left on the stone by nearly
2,000 years of weather, it could have been built yesterday.
Behind the wall, scooped out of a hillside whose slope lends
itself naturally to stepped seating, curved banks of stone can
accommodate about 10,000 spectators.

Originally, they were seated according to class: magistrates and local senators in the front, priests and members of the trading guilds behind them, then the man in the street and his wife and finally, high up and far away from respectable folk, the *pullati*, or beggars and prostitutes. By 1990, the rules had changed, and the allocation of seats depended not so much on class as speed off the mark. The concert was a foregone sellout; swift and decisive action was necessary to secure tickets.

It was taken, while we were still dithering, by our friend Christopher, a man who operates with military precision when it comes to the big night out. He arranged everything, and gave us our marching orders: on parade at 1800 hours, dinner in Orange under a magnolia tree at 1930 hours, seated in the theatre by 2100 hours. All ranks to be equipped with cushions to protect buttocks from stone seats. Liquid rations provided for the intermission. Return to base approximately 0100 hours.

There are times when it is a relief and a pleasure to be told exactly what to do, and this was one of them. We left at six sharp, arriving in Orange an hour later to find the town in festival mood. Every café was full and bustling, with extra tables and chairs edging out into the streets to make driving a test of how many waiters you could avoid bumping into. Already, more than two hours before the performance, hundreds of people with cushions and picnic baskets were streaming towards the theatre. The restaurants displayed special menus for the *soirée* Pavarotti. *Le tout* Orange was rubbing its hands in anticipation. And then it started to rain.

The whole town looked upwards – waiters, drivers, cushion-carriers and no doubt the maestro himself – as the first few drops landed on dusty streets that had been dry for weeks. *Quelle catastrophe!* Would he sing under an umbrella? How could the orchestra play with damp instruments, the conductor conduct with a dripping baton? For as long as the shower lasted, you could almost feel thousands of people holding their breath.

But by nine o'clock, the rain had long since gone and the first stars were coming out above the immense wall of the theatre as we joined the scrum of music-lovers and shuffled past the display of Pavarottiana on sale beside the entrance. Compact discs, tapes, posters, T-shirts – all the products of pop merchandising were there apart from I Love Luciano bumper stickers.

The line kept stopping, as though there were an obstruction beyond the entrance, and when we came through into the theatre I realized why. You stood still – you had to stand still – for a few seconds to take in the view from the front of the stage, the view that Pavarotti would see.

Thousands and thousands of faces, pale against the darkness, made row after blurred row of semi-circles which disappeared up into the night. From ground level, there was a feeling of reverse vertigo. The angle of the seating seemed impossibly steep, the spectators perched and precarious, on the brink of losing their balance and toppling down into the pit. The sound they made was uncanny – above a whisper, but below normal speech, a continuous, quiet buzz of conversation that was contained and magnified by the stone walls. I felt as though I had stepped into a human beehive.

We climbed to our seats, 100 feet or so above the stage, exactly opposite a niche high in the wall where a floodlit statue of Augustus Caesar, in his imperial toga, stood with his arm outstretched to the crowd. In his day, the population of Orange had been about 85,000; it is now fewer than 30,000, and most of them seemed to be trying to find a few spare inches of stone to sit on.

A woman of operatic girth, blowing hard after scaling the steps, collapsed on her cushion next to me and fanned herself with a programme. She was from Orange, round-faced and jolly, and she had been many times to the theatre before. But she had never seen an audience like this, she said. She surveyed the heads and made her calculations: 13,000 people, she was sure of it. *Dieu merci* that the rain had stopped.

There was a sudden crack of applause as the members of the orchestra filed on stage and began to tune up, musical fragments that came sharp and clear through the expectant hum of the crowd. With a closing rumble from the kettle drums, the orchestra stopped, and looked, as everyone in the theatre looked, towards the back of the stage. Directly below the statue of Augustus, the central entrance had been draped with black curtains. The rows of heads around us leant forward in unison, as though they'd been rehearsed, and from behind the black curtain came the black and white figure of the conductor.

Another explosion of hands, and a shrill, ragged chorus of whistles from the seats far behind and above us. Madame next door tut-tutted. This was not a football match. *Épouvantable* behaviour. In fact, it was probably in accordance with tradition, since the whistling was coming from the beggars' and prostitutes' seats, not an area where one would expect to hear genteel applause.

The orchestra played a Donizetti overture, the music floating and dipping in the night air, undistorted and naturally amplified, bathing the theatre in sound. The acoustics were mercilessly revealing. If there were any false notes tonight, most of Orange would know.

The conductor bowed and walked back towards the curtain, and there was a moment – hardly more than a second – when 13,000 people were silent. And then, to a roar that must have felt like a physical blow, the man himself appeared, black hair, black beard, white tie and tails, a voluminous white handkerchief floating from his left hand. He spread his arms to the crowd. He put his palms together and bowed his head. Pavarotti was ready to sing.

Up in the beggars' and prostitutes' section, however, they were not ready to stop whistling – piercing, two fingers in the mouth whistles that could have hailed a taxi on the other side of Orange. Madame next door was scandalized. Opera hooligans, she called them. *Shhhh*, she went. *Shhhh*, went thousands of others. Renewed whistling from the beggars and prostitutes. Pavarotti stood waiting, head down, arms by his side. The conductor's baton was up. To the accompaniment of a few last defiant whistles, they began.

'*Quanto è cara, quanto è bella*,' sang Pavarotti. It sounded so easy, the size of his voice reducing the theatre to the size of a room. He stood very still, his weight on his right leg, the heel of his left foot raised slightly from the ground, handkerchief rippling in the breeze – a relaxed, perfectly controlled performance.

He finished with a ritual that he would repeat throughout the evening: an upward flick of the head at the end of the final note, a vast grin, arms spread wide before bringing his palms together and bowing his head, a handshake with the conductor while the applause thundered down to crash against the back wall.

He sang again, and before the applause had died away he was escorted by the conductor to the curtained entrance and disappeared. I imagined he had gone to rest his vocal chords and have a restorative spoonful of honey. But Madame next door had a different explanation, and it intrigued me for the next two hours.

'*À mon avis,*' she said, 'he is taking a light dinner between arias.'

'Surely not, Madame,' I said.

'*Shhh.* Here is the flautist.'

At the end of the piece, Madame returned to her theory. Pavarotti, she said, was a big man and a famous gourmet. The performance was long. To sing as he sang, *comme un ange,* was hard, demanding work. It was altogether logical that he should sustain himself during the periods when he was not on stage. If I were to study the programme, I would see that it might have been constructed to allow for a well-spaced six-course snack to be consumed while the orchestra diverted the audience. *Voilà!*

I looked at the programme, and I had to admit that Madame had a point. It was entirely possible, and reading between the arias, a menu appeared:

DONIZETTI
(*Insalata di carciofi*)

CILEA
(*Zuppa di fagioli alla Toscana*)

ENTRACTE
(*Sogliole alla Veneziana*)

PUCCINI
(*Tonnelini con funghi e piselli*)

VERDI
(Formaggi)

MASSENET
(Granita di limone)

ENCORE
(Caffè e grappa)

There was another, more visible sign that the singing supper might not be just a figment of Madame's imagination. Like everyone else, I had assumed that the white square draped elegantly through the fingers of Pavarotti's left hand was a handkerchief. But it was larger than a handkerchief, much larger. I mentioned it to Madame, and she nodded. '*Évidemment*,' she said, '*c'est une serviette*.' Having proved her case, she settled back to enjoy the rest of the concert.

Pavarotti was unforgettable, not only for his singing but for the way in which he played to the audience, risking the occasional vocal departure from the score, patting the conductor on the cheek when it came off, making his exits and entrances with faultless timing. After one of his periods behind the curtain, he returned wearing a long blue scarf wrapped round his neck and reaching to his waist – against the cool night air, or so I thought.

Madame, of course, knew better. He has had a small accident with some sauce, she said, and the scarf is there to conceal the spots on his white waistcoat. Isn't he divine?

The official programme ended, but the orchestra lingered on. From the beggars' and prostitutes' section came an insistent chant – *Ver-di! Ver-di! Ver-di!* – and this time it spread through the crowd until Pavarotti emerged to give us a second helping of encores: *Nessun Dorma, O Sole Mio*, rapture in the audience, bows from the orchestra, one last salute from the star and then it was over.

It took us half an hour to clear the exit, and as we came out we saw two enormous Mercedes pulling away from the theatre. 'I bet that's him,' said Christopher. 'I wonder where he's going to have dinner.' He wasn't to know, because he hadn't been sitting next to Madame, what had been going on behind the black curtain. Thirteen thousand people had been to dinner with Pavarotti without realizing it. I hope he comes to Orange again, and I hope that next time they print the menu in the programme.

15

A Pastis Lesson

Tin tables and scuffed wicker chairs are set out under the shade of massive plane trees. It is close to noon, and the motes of dust kicked up by an old man's canvas boots as he shuffles across the square hang for a long moment in the air, sharply defined in the glare of the sun. The café waiter looks up from his copy of *L'Équipe* and saunters out to take your order.

He comes back with a small glass, maybe a quarter full if he's been generous, and a beaded carafe of water. The glass turns cloudy as you fill it up, a colour somewhere between yellow and misty grey, and there is the sharp, sweet smell of aniseed.

Santé. You are drinking *pastis*, the milk of Provence.

For me, the most powerful ingredient in *pastis* is not aniseed or alcohol, but *ambiance*, and that dictates how and where it should be drunk. I cannot imagine drinking it in a hurry. I cannot imagine drinking it in a pub in Fulham, a bar in New York, or anywhere that requires its customers to wear socks. It wouldn't taste the same. There has to be heat and sunlight and the illusion that the clock has stopped. I have to be in Provence.

Before moving here, I had always thought of *pastis* as a commodity, a French national asset made by two giant institutions. There was Pernod, there was Ricard, and that was it.

Then I started to come across others – Casanis, Janot, Granier – and I wondered how many different *marques* there were. I counted five in one bar, seven in another. Every Provençal I asked was, of course, an expert. Each of them gave me a different, emphatic and probably inaccurate answer, complete with disparaging remarks about the brands that he personally wouldn't give to his mother-in-law.

It was only by chance that I found a professor of *pastis*, and since he also happens to be a very good chef, attending class was no hardship.

Michel Bosc was born near Avignon and emigrated to Cabrières, a few miles away. For twelve years now, he has run a restaurant in the village, *Le Bistrot à Michel*, and each year he has put his profits back into the business. He has added a large terrace, expanded the kitchens, put in four bedrooms for over-tired or over-indulged customers, and generally turned *chez* Michel into a comfortable, bustling place.

But despite all the improvements, and the occasional outbreaks of rampant chic among the summer clientele, one thing hasn't changed. The bar at the front of the restaurant is still the village bar. Every evening there will be half a dozen men with burnt faces and work clothes who have dropped in, not to eat, but to argue about *boules* over a couple of drinks. And the drinks are invariably *pastis*.

We arrived one evening to find Michel behind the bar, presiding over an informal *dégustation*. Seven or eight different brands were being put through their paces by the local enthusiasts, some of them brands I had never seen.

A *pastis* tasting is not the hushed, almost religious ritual that you might find in the cellars of Bordeaux or Burgundy, and Michel had to raise his voice to make himself heard over the smacking of lips and the banging of glasses on the bar.

'Try this,' he said. 'It's just like mother used to make. It comes from Forcalquier.' He slid a glass across the bar and topped it up from a sweating metal jug rattling with ice cubes.

I sipped. This is what mother used to make? Two or three of these and I'd be lucky to make it upstairs to one of the bedrooms on my hands and knees. I said it seemed strong, and Michel showed me the bottle: 45 degrees of alcohol, stronger than brandy, but not above the legal limit for *pastis*, and positively mild in comparison with one that Michel had once been given. Two of those, he said, would make a man fall straight backwards with a smile on his face, *plof!* But it was something special, that one, and I gathered from Michel's half-wink that it was not altogether legal.

He left the bar suddenly, as if he'd remembered a *soufflé* in the oven, and came back with some objects that he put in front of me on the bar.

'Do you know what those are?'

There was a tall, spiral-patterned glass on a short, thick stem; a smaller, chunky glass, as narrow as a thimble and twice as high; and what looked like a flattened tin spoon decorated with symmetrical rows of perforations. On the stem just behind the flat head was a U-shaped kink.

'This place used to be a café long before I took it over,' said Michel. 'I found these when we were knocking through a wall. You've never seen them before?'

I had no idea what they were.

'In the old days, all the cafés had them. They're for

absinthe.' He curled an index finger round the end of his nose and twisted, the gesture for drunkenness. He picked up the smaller of the two glasses. 'This is the *dosette*, the old measure for *absinthe.*' It was solid and tactile, and felt as heavy as a slug of lead when he passed it to me. He took the other glass and balanced the spoon on top of it, the kink in the stem fitting snugly over the rim.

'*Bon*. On here' – he tapped the blade of the spoon – 'you put sugar. Then you pour water over the sugar and it drips through the holes and into the *absinthe*. At the end of the last century, this was a drink very much *à la mode*.'

Absinthe, so Michel told me, was a green liqueur originally distilled from wine and the wormwood plant. Very bitter, stimulating and hallucinogenic, addictive and dangerous. It was nearly 70 degrees of alcohol, and could cause blindness, epilepsy and insanity. Under its influence, Van Gogh is said to have cut off his own ear, and Verlaine to have shot Rimbaud. It gave its name to a particular disease – *absinthisme* – and the addict would quite often '*casser sa pipe*' and die. For this reason, it was made illegal in 1915.

One man who would not have been pleased to see it go was Jules Pernod, who had an *absinthe* factory at Montfavet, near Avignon. But he adapted to the times by changing his production over to a drink based on the legally authorized *anis*. It was an immediate success, with the considerable advantage that customers would live to come back for more.

'So you see,' said Michel, 'commercial *pastis* was born in Avignon, like me. Try another one.'

He took a bottle of Granier from the shelf, and I was able to say that I had the same brand at home. Granier, '*Mon pastis*' as it says on the label, is made in Cavaillon. It has a more gentle colour than Pernod's rather fierce greenish tinge, and I find it a softer drink. Also, I'm inclined to support local endeavours whenever they taste good.

The Granier went down and I was still standing up. To continue my first lesson, Michel said, it was necessary to try another, a *grande marque*, so that I could make a considered judgement across a range of slight variations in taste and colour. He gave me a Ricard.

By this time, it was becoming rather difficult to maintain a detached and scholarly attitude to the comparison of one *pastis* against another. I liked them all – clean-tasting, smooth and insidious. One might have had a drop more licorice than the rest, but the palate develops a certain numbness after a few highly flavoured and highly alcoholic shots. It's a pleasant numbness, and it stimulates a roaring appetite, but any traces of critical appraisal I might have started with had vanished somewhere between the second and third glasses. As a *pastis* connoisseur, I was hopeless. Happy and hungry, but hopeless.

'How was the Ricard?' asked Michel. I said that the Ricard was fine, but perhaps I had absorbed enough education for one night.

For days afterwards, I kept scribbling down questions that I wanted to ask Michel. I found it curious, for instance, that the word was so well known and had such strong associations, and yet its origins seemed as cloudy as the drink itself. Who had invented *pastis* before Pernod had taken it over? Why was it so firmly rooted in Provence, rather than Burgundy or the Loire? I went back to the professor.

Whenever I have asked a Provençal about Provence – whether about climate, food, history, the habits of animals or the oddities of humans – I have never been short of answers. The Provençal loves to instruct, usually with a great deal of personal embroidery, and preferably around a table. And so it was this time. Michel arranged a lunch, on the one day of the week when his restaurant is normally closed, with a few friends he described as '*hommes responsables*' who would be happy to lead me down the path of knowledge.

Eighteen of us gathered under the big white canvas umbrella in Michel's courtyard, and I was introduced to a blur of faces and names and descriptions: a government official from Avignon, a wine grower from Carpentras, two executives from Ricard, some stalwarts from Cabrières. There was even a man wearing a tie, but he slipped it off after five minutes and hung it in a noose over a drinks trolley. That was the beginning and the end of any formality.

Most of the men shared Michel's passion for *boules*, and the wine grower from Carpentras had brought with him a few cases of his special *cuvée*, with labels showing a game in progress. While the *rosé* was being chilled and the red uncorked, there was a generous dispensation of the sporting drink and the *boules*-player's standby, *le vrai pastis de Marseille, le pastis Ricard*.

Born in 1909 and, according to one of his executives, still looking for trouble, Paul Ricard's success is a classic case of energetic and intelligent exploitation. His father was a wine merchant, and young Paul's work took him into the bars and *bistrots* of Marseille. In those days, the laws of concoction were not stringent, and many bars made their own *pastis*. Ricard decided to make his, but he added an ingredient that the others lacked, which was a genius for promotion. *Le vrai pastis de Marseille* may not have been very different from the others, but it was good, and made better by Ricard's talent for marketing. It was not long before his *pastis* was the most popular *pastis*, at least in Marseille.

Ricard was ready to expand, and he made a decision that probably accelerated his success by several years. The area round Marseille was a competitive market; *pastis* was everywhere, a commonplace drink. And Marseille itself didn't enjoy the best of reputations among its neighbours. (Even today, a Marseillais is regarded as a *blagueur*, an exaggerator, a man who will describe a sardine as a whale, not entirely to be believed.)

Further north, however, *pastis* could be sold as something exotic, and distance lent improvement to Marseille's reputation. It could be invested with the charm of the south – a slightly raffish, relaxed, sunny charm which would appeal to a northerner used to freezing winters and grey skies. So Ricard went north, first to Lyon and then to Paris, and the formula worked. Today, it would be unusual to find a bar anywhere in France without its bottle of *le vrai pastis de Marseille*.

The man from Ricard who was telling me this talked about his *patron* with genuine liking. Monsieur Paul, he said, was *un original*, someone who looked for a challenge every day. When I asked if he was involved, like many powerful businessmen, in politics, there was a snort of laughter. 'Politicians? He vomits on them all.' I had some sympathy for the sentiment, but in a way I thought it was a pity. The idea of a *pastis* baron as President of France appealed to me, and he would probably have been elected on his advertising slogan: *Un Ricard, sinon rien*.

But Ricard hadn't invented *pastis*. Like Pernod, he had bottled and marketed something that had been there before. Where had it come from? Who had first mixed the *anis*, the licorice, the sugar and the alcohol? Was there a monk (monks, for some reason, have an affinity for alcoholic invention, from champagne to Benedictine) who had made the discovery one blessed day in the monastery kitchens?

Nobody around the table knew exactly how the first glass of *pastis* had come into a thirsty world, but lack of precise knowledge never inhibits a Provençal from expressing an opinion as fact, or a legend as reliable history. The least plausible, and therefore favourite, explanation was the hermit theory – hermits, of course, being almost up to monk standard when it comes to the invention of unusual *apéritifs*.

This particular hermit lived in a hut deep in the forest on the slopes of the Lubéron. He collected herbs, which he stewed in a giant pot, the traditional bubbling cauldron favoured by witches, wizards and alchemists. The juices left in the cauldron after boiling had remarkable properties, not only quenching the hermit's thirst, but protecting him from an outbreak of plague that was threatening to decimate the population of the Lubéron. The hermit was a generous fellow, and shared his mixture with sufferers from the plague, who immediately recovered. Sensing, perhaps like Paul Ricard long after him, the wider possibilities for his miraculous drink, he left his forest hut and did what any businesslike hermit would have done: he moved to Marseille and opened a bar.

The less picturesque but more likely reason for Provence being the home of *pastis* is that the ingredients were easy to come by. The herbs were cheap, or free. Most peasants made their own wine and distilled their own head-splitting liqueurs, and until fairly recently the right of distillation was a family asset that could be passed down from father to son. That right has been revoked, but there are some surviving *distillateurs* who, until they die, are legally entitled to make what they drink, and *pastis maison* still exists.

Madame Bosc, Michel's wife, was born near Carpentras and remembers her grandfather making a double-strength *pastis*, illegally alcoholic, a drink that could make a statue fall down. One day grandfather received a visit from the village *gendarme*. An official visit, on the official *moto*, in full uniform, never a good sign. The *gendarme* was persuaded into one of grandfather's virulent glasses of *pastis*; then another, then a third. The purpose of the visit was never discussed, but grandfather had to make two trips to the *gendarmerie* in his van. The first was to deliver the unconscious policeman and his bike; the second, to deliver his boots and his *pistolet*, which had been discovered later under the table.

Those were the days. And somewhere in Provence, they probably still are.

16

Inside the Belly of Avignon

Place Pie, in the centre of Avignon, is a forlorn sight in the dingy grey moments that come just before dawn. It is an architectural mongrel of a square, with two sides of seedy but elegant old buildings looking across at a hideous monument to modern town planning. A graduate of the *béton armé* school of construction has been given a free hand with the concrete, and he has made the worst of it.

Benches, crude slabs, have been dumped around a central eyesore. On those benches, the weary sightseer can rest and contemplate a second, much more imposing eyesore, three stained concrete stories which on weekdays are crammed with cars by eight in the morning. The reason for the cars, and the reason I was in Place Pie in time to see dawn's rosy flush come up on the concrete, is that the best food in Avignon is displayed and sold under the car park, in *Les Halles*.

I arrived there a few minutes before six and parked in one of the few free places on the second level. Below me on the *place*, I saw two derelicts with skin the same colour as the bench they were sitting on. They were sharing a litre of red wine, taking turns to swig from the bottle. A *gendarme* came up to them and gestured them to move on, then stood with his hands on his hips, watching. They walked in the slouched, defeated way of men with nothing to hope for and nowhere to go, and sat on the pavement on the other side of the *place*. The *gendarme* shrugged and turned away.

The contrast between the quiet, dull emptiness of the *place* and the interior of *Les Halles* was sudden and total. On one side of the door was a town still asleep; on the other, bright lights and bright colours, pandemonium and shouting and laughter, a working day in full and noisy swing.

I had to jump aside to avoid collision with a trolley piled to head height with crates of peaches, pushed by a man chanting '*Klaxon! Klaxon!*' as he careered round the corner. Other trolleys were behind him, their loads swaying. I looked for somewhere to escape from high-velocity fruit and vege-tables, and made a dash for a sign that read *buvette*. If I was going to be run over, I would rather the tragedy occurred at a bar.

Jacky and Isabelle, so the sign said, were the owners, and they were in a state of siege. The bar was so crowded that three men were reading the same newspaper, and all the tables nearby were taken up with the first sitting for break-fast, or possibly lunch. It was difficult to tell by looking at the food which meal was being eaten. *Croissants* were being dipped into thick, steaming cups of *café crème* next to tum-blers of red wine and sausage sandwiches as long as a forearm, or beer and crusty squares of warm pizza. I felt a twinge of longing for the breakfast of champions, the half pint of red wine and the sausage sandwich, but drinking at dawn is the reward for working all night. I ordered coffee, and tried to see some semblance of order in the surrounding chaos.

Les Halles take up an area perhaps seventy yards square, and very few inches are wasted. Three main passageways separate the *étaux*, stalls of varying sizes, and at that time in the morning it was hard to imagine customers being able to reach them. Crates, mangled cardboard boxes and wispy clumps of paper straw were stacked high in front of many of the counters, and the floor was garnished with casualties – lettuce leaves, squashed tomatoes, errant *haricots* – that had been unable to cling on during the last breakneck stage of delivery.

The stallholders, too busy writing up the day's prices and arranging their produce to spare five minutes for a visit to the bar, bellowed for coffee, which was served to them by Isabelle's waitress, an acrobatic girl over the crates and a steady hand with her tray. She even managed to keep her footing in the high-risk zone of the fish-sellers, where the floor was slick with the ice that men with raw, nicked hands and rubber aprons were shovelling on to the steel display shelves.

It made a noise like gravel on glass, and there was another, more painful sound that cut through the hubbub as the butchers sawed at bones and severed tendons with decisive, dangerously fast chops of their cleavers. I hoped for their fingers' sake that they hadn't had wine for breakfast.

After half an hour it was safe to leave the bar. The piles of crates had been removed, the trolleys parked, the traffic was on legs now instead of wheels. An army of brooms had whisked away the scraps of fallen vegetables, prices had been marked on spiked plastic labels, tills unlocked, coffee drunk. *Les Halles* were open for business.

I have never seen so much fresh food and so much variety in such a confined space. I counted fifty stalls, many of them entirely devoted to a single speciality. There were two stalls selling olives – just olives – in every conceivable style of preparation: olives *à la grecque*, olives in herb-flavoured oil, olives mixed with scarlet shards of pimento, olives from Nyons, olives from Les Baux, olives that looked like small black plums or elongated green grapes. They were lined up in squat wooden tubs, gleaming as though each one had been individually polished. At the end of the line were the only non-olives to be seen, a barrel of anchovies from Collioure, packed in tighter than any sardines, sharp and salty when I leant down to smell them. Madame behind the counter told me to try one, with a plump black olive. Did I know how to make *tapenade*, the olive and anchovy paste? A pot of that every day and I'd live to be a hundred.

Another stall, another specialist: anything with feathers. Pigeons, plucked and trussed, capons, breasts of duck and thighs of duckling, three different members of the chicken aristocracy, with the supreme chickens, the *poulets de Bresse*, wearing their red, white and blue labels like medals. *Légalement contrôlée*, said the labels, by the *Comité Interprofessionel de la Volaille de Bresse*. I could imagine the chosen chickens receiving their decorations from a dignified committee member, almost certainly with the traditional kiss on each side of the beak.

And then there were fish, laid out gill to gill on a row of stalls that extended along the length of one wall, forty yards or more of glistening scales and still-bright eyes. Banks of crushed ice, smelling of the sea, separated the squid from the blood-darkened tuna, the *rascasses* from the *loups de mer*, the cod from the skate. Pyramids of clams, of the molluscs called *seiches*, of winkles, tiny grey shrimp and monster *gambas*, fish for *friture*, fish for *soupe*, lobsters the colour of dark steel, jolts of yellow coming from the dishes of fresh lemons on the counter, deft hands with long thin knives cutting and gutting, the squelch of rubber boots on the wet stone floor.

It was coming up to seven o'clock, and the first housewives were starting to investigate, with prods and squeezes, what they would be cooking that night. The market opens at 5.30, and the first half hour is officially reserved for the *commerçants* and restaurant owners, but I couldn't see anyone being courageous enough to stand in the way of a determined Avignon matron who wanted to get her errands done before six. Shop early for the best, we had often been told, and wait until just before the market closes for the cheapest.

But who could wait that long, surrounded by temptation like this? In one short stretch, I had mentally eaten a dozen times. A bowl of brown free-range eggs turned into a *piperade*, with Bayonne ham from the stall next door and peppers a few feet further on. That kept me going until I reached the smoked salmon and caviar. But there were the cheeses, the *saucissons*, the rabbit and hare and pork *pâtés*, the great pale scoops of *rillettes*, the *confits de canard* – it would be madness not to try them all.

I very nearly stopped my researches to have a picnic in the car park. Everything I needed – including bread from one stall, wine from another – was within twenty yards, fresh and beautifully presented. What could have been a better way to start the day? I realized that my appetite had adjusted to the environment, leapfrogging several hours. My watch said 7.30. My stomach whispered lunch, and to hell with the time. I went to look for the liquid moral support of more coffee.

There are three bars in *Les Halles* – Jacky and Isabelle, Cyrille and Evelyne and, the most dangerous of the three,

Chez Kiki, where they start serving champagne long before most people get up. I saw two burly men toasting each other, their *flûtes* of champagne held delicately between thick fingers, earth under their fingernails, earth on their heavy boots. Obviously, they had sold their lettuces well that morning.

The passageways and stalls were now crowded with members of the public, shopping with the intent, slightly suspicious expressions of people who were determined to find the most tender, the juiciest, the best. A woman put on her reading glasses to inspect a row of cauliflowers which, to me, looked identical. She picked one up, hefted it in her hand, peered at its tight white head, sniffed it, put it down. Three times she did this before making her choice, and then she watched the stallholder over the top of her glasses to make sure he didn't try to substitute it for a less perfect specimen in the back row. I remembered being told not to handle the vegetables in a London greengrocer's. There would have been outrage here if the same miserable ruling were introduced. No fruit or vegetables are bought without going through trial by touch, and any stallholder who tried to discourage the habit would be pelted out of the market.

Avignon has had its *Halles* since 1910, although the site under the car park has only been in operation since 1973. That was as much information as the girl in the office could give me. When I asked about the amount of food sold in a day or a week, she just shrugged and told me *beaucoup.*

And *beaucoup* there certainly was, being stuffed and piled into every kind of receptacle from battered suitcases to handbags seemingly capable of infinite expansion. An elderly, bandy-legged man in shorts and a crash helmet wheeled his Mobylette up to the entrance and came in to collect his morning's shopping – a plastic *cageot* of melons and peaches, two enormous baskets straining to contain their contents, a cotton sack with a dozen *baguettes*. He distributed the weight carefully around his machine. The crate of fruit was secured with elastic straps to the rack behind the saddle, the baskets hung on the handlebars, the bread sack slung across his back. As he wheeled his load – enough food for a week – away from the market, he shouted at one of the stallholders, '*À demain!*'

I watched him as he joined the traffic in the Place Pie, the tiny engine of his bike spluttering with effort, his head bent foward over the handlebars and the *baguettes* sticking up like a quiver of fat golden arrows. It was eleven o'clock, and the café opposite the market had tables on the pavement set for lunch.

17

Postcards from Summer

It has taken us three years to accept the fact that we live in the same house, but in two different places.

What we think of as normal life starts in September. Apart from market days in the towns, there are no crowds. Traffic on the back roads is sparse during the day – a tractor, a few vans – and virtually non-existent at night. There is always a table in every restaurant, except perhaps for Sunday lunch. Social life is intermittent and uncomplicated. The baker has bread, the plumber has time for a chat, the postman has time for a drink. After the first deafening weekend of the hunting season, the forest is quiet. Each field has a stooped, reflective figure working among the vines, very slowly up one line, very slowly down the next. The hours between noon and two are dead.

And then we come to July and August.

We used to treat them as just another two months of the year; hot months, certainly, but nothing that required much adjustment on our part except to make sure that the after-noon included a siesta.

We were wrong. Where we live in July and August is still the Lubéron, but it's not the same Lubéron. It is the Lubéron *en vacances*, and our past efforts to live normally during abnormal times have been miserably unsuccessful. So unsuccessful that we once considered cancelling summer altogether and going somewhere grey and cool and peaceful, like the Hebrides.

But if we did, we would probably miss it, all of it, even the days and incidents that have reduced us to sweating, irritated, over-tired zombies. So we have decided to come to terms with the Lubéron in the summer, to do our best to join the rest of the world on holiday and, like them, to send postcards telling distant friends about the wonderful times we are having. Here are a few.

Marignane airport

Three in the afternoon, and still no sign of the one o'clock plane.

When I called to confirm that it was on time, I was given the standard optimistic lie. And so I left home at 11.30 and spent the hottest hour of a hot day on the *autoroute*, trying to avoid sudden death among a swarm of Renault 5 missiles launched early that morning from Paris and targeted on the Côte d'Azur. How can these people steer with all four wheels off the ground?

Un petit retard is indicated on the flight arrivals board, nothing much, forty-five minutes. Time for coffee, two coffees. The flights to Oran have been delayed too, and the airport lounge is carpeted with Arab workmen and their families going home, the children nesting among overstuffed plastic suitcases striped in blue and pink and white. The expressions on the dark, seamed faces of the men are patient and resigned.

The girl at the desk answers my question about the flight by pointing at the board: forty-five minutes late. When I say that the plane is already an hour late, she shrugs and consults the crystal ball in her computer. Yes, it is as the board indicates, forty-five minutes late. Has the plane left London yet? Yes, she says. But I know she's been trained in deception like all the rest of them.

It is just before five when the plane gets in and the pale-faced, bad-tempered passengers begin to come through. The first hours of their holiday have been spent sitting on the tarmac at Heathrow. Some of them make the mistake of slapping their passports down impatiently on the counter in front of the immigration officer. He takes his revenge by examining each page with painstaking, exasperating thoroughness, pausing between pages to lick the tip of his finger.

My friends come through, looking rumpled but cheerful. A few minutes to pick up the bags and then we can be back in plenty of time for a swim before dinner. But a quarter of an hour later they are still waiting in the deserted baggage claim area. The airline has made separate holiday arrangements for one of their suitcases – Newcastle, Hong Kong, who knows? – and we join the other castaways in Lost Luggage.

We are home by 7.30, almost exactly eight hours after I left.

Saint-Tropez

Cherchez les nudistes! It is open season for nature-lovers, and there is likely to be a sharp increase in the number of applicants wishing to join the Saint-Tropez police force.

The mayor, Monsieur Spada, has decreed that in the name of safety and hygiene there will be no more naked sunbathing on the public beaches. '*Le nudisme intégral est interdit,*' says Monsieur Spada, and he has empowered the police to seize and arrest any offenders. Well, perhaps not to seize them, but to track them down and fine them 75 francs, or as much as 1,500 francs if they have been guilty of creating a public outrage. Exactly where a nudist might keep 1,500 francs is a question that is puzzling local residents.

Meanwhile, a defiant group of nudists has set up headquarters in some rocks behind *la plage de la Moutte*. A spokeswoman for the group has said that under no circumstances would bathing suits be worn. Wish you were here.

The melon field

Faustin's brother Jacky, a wiry little man of sixty or so, grows melons in the field opposite the house. It's a large field, but he does all the work himself, and by hand. In the spring I have often seen him out there for six or seven hours, back bent like a hinge, his hoe chopping at the weeds that threaten to strangle his crop. He doesn't spray – who would eat a melon tasting of chemicals? – and I think he must enjoy looking after his land in the traditional way.

Now that the melons are ripening, he comes to the field at six every morning to pick the ones that are ready. He takes them up to Ménerbes to be packed in shallow wooden crates. From Ménerbes they go to Cavaillon, and from Cavaillon to Avignon, to Paris, everywhere. It amuses Jacky to think of people in smart restaurants paying *une petite fortune* for a simple thing like a melon.

If I get up early enough I can catch him before he goes to Ménerbes. He always has a couple of melons that are too ripe to travel, and he sells them to me for a few francs.

As I walk back to the house, the sun clears the top of the mountain and it is suddenly hot on my face. The melons, heavy and satisfying in my hands, are still cool from the night air. We have them for breakfast, fresh and sweet, less than ten minutes after they have been picked.

Behind the bar

There is a point at which a swimming pool ceases to be a luxury and becomes very close to a necessity, and that point is when the temperature hits 100 degrees. Whenever people ask us about renting a house for the summer, we always tell them this, and some of them listen.

Others don't, and within two days of arriving they are on the phone telling us what we told them months before. It's so *hot*, they say. Too hot for tennis, too hot for cycling, too hot for sightseeing, too hot, too hot. Oh for a pool. You're so lucky.

There is a hopeful pause. Is it my imagination, or can I actually hear the drops of perspiration falling like summer rain on the pages of the telephone directory?

I suppose the answer is to be callous but helpful. There is a public swimming pool near Apt, if you don't mind sharing the water with a few hundred small brown dervishes on their school holidays. There is the Mediterranean, only an hour's drive away; no, with traffic it could take two hours. Make sure you have some bottles of Évian in the car. It wouldn't do to get dehydrated.

Or you could close the shutters against the sun, spend the

day in the house and spring forth refreshed into the evening air. It would be difficult to acquire the souvenir suntan, but at least there would be no chance of heatstroke.

These brutal and unworthy suggestions barely have time to cross my mind before the voice of despair turns into the voice of relief. Of course! We could come over in the morning for a quick dip without disturbing you. Just a splash. You won't even know we've been.

They come at noon, with friends. They swim. They take the sun. Thirst creeps up on them, much to their surprise, and that's why I'm behind the bar. My wife is in the kitchen, making lunch for six. *Vivent les vacances.*

The night walk

The dogs cope with the heat by sleeping through it, stretched out in the courtyard or curled in the shade of the rosemary hedge. They come to life as the pink in the sky is turning to darkness, sniffing the breeze, jostling each other around our feet in their anticipation of a walk. We take the torch and follow them into the forest.

It smells of warm pine needles and baked earth, dry and spicy when we step on a patch of thyme. Small, invisible creatures slither away from us and rustle through the leaves of the wild box that grows like a weed.

Sounds carry: *cigales* and frogs, the muffled thump of music through the open window of a faraway house, the clinks and murmurs of dinner drifting up from Faustin's terrace. The hills on the other side of the valley, uninhabited for ten months a year, are pricked with lights that will be switched off at the end of August.

We get back to the house and take off our shoes, and the warmth of the flagstones is an invitation to swim. A dive into dark water, and then a last glass of wine. The sky is clear except for a jumble of stars; it will be hot again tomorrow. Hot and slow, just like today.

A slight mechanical problem

Our friend had decided to trade in her old car for a new one, and the young car salesman was determined to give her the benefit of his sales pitch. Dapper in a suit despite the heat, he pranced around the new car, pointing out its various attractions with elaborate flourishes, shooting his cuffs and rattling his jewellery.

Our friend endured this with as much patience as she could summon up, and then suggested that a test drive might be a practical way of judging the car's many virtues.

Of course, said the salesman, *mais attention!* He removed his sunglasses for emphasis. This model is very much more *nerveuse* than yours. When I drove it here today, even I was impressed. One touch on the accelerator and you are flying. You will see.

After much meticulous adjustment of the driving position and a final warning about the incredible velocity that was waiting to be unleashed, our friend was presented with the ignition key.

The engine coughed once, and died. Second and third attempts were no more successful. The smile on the salesman's face faded. The car obviously needed a man's touch. He took over in the driving seat and failed to start the car. *Incroyable!* What can be the problem? He opened the bonnet and looked at the engine. He burrowed under the dashboard searching for a loose connection.

Was it at all possible, our friend asked, that the car needed petrol? The salesman tried to hide the scorn he felt for empty-headed women who ask such ridiculous questions, but to humour her turned the key again and inspected the fuel gauge. Drier than dry. He flounced out of the car. Unfortunately, as this was a small showroom and not a garage, petrol was not available on the premises. Another rendezvous would have to be arranged for the test drive. Could Madame come back this afternoon? No? *Merde.*

The desire to conclude the sale overcame the heat and the loss of face, and the young man in the dapper suit had to walk half a mile up the N100 to borrow a jerrican of petrol from the nearest garage, leaving our friend in charge of the showroom. She made a joke about bringing her own petrol next time she wanted to buy a car, which was not well received.

Knee-deep in lavender

I had been cutting lavender with a pair of secateurs and I was making a slow, amateurish job of it, nearly an hour to do fewer than a dozen clumps. When Henriette arrived at the house with a basket of aubergines, I was pleased to have the chance to stop.

Henriette looked at the lavender, looked at the secateurs and shook her head at the ignorance of her neighbour. Didn't I know how to cut lavender? What was I doing with those secateurs? Where was my *faucille*?

She went to her van and came back with a blackened

sickle, its needle tip embedded in an old wine cork for safety. It was surprisingly light, and felt sharp enough to shave with. I made a few passes with it in the air, and Henriette shook her head again. Obviously, I needed a lesson.

She hitched up her skirt and attacked the nearest row of lavender, gathering the long stems into a tight bunch with one arm and slicing them off at the bottom with a single smooth pull of the sickle. In five minutes she had cut more than I had in an hour. It looked easy; bend, gather, pull. Nothing to it.

'*Voilà!*' said Henriette. 'When I was a little girl in the Basses Alpes, we had hectares of lavender, and no machines. Everyone used the *faucille*.'

She passed it back to me, told me to mind my legs and went off to join Faustin in the vines.

It wasn't as easy as it looked, and my first effort produced a ragged, uneven clump, more chewed than sliced. I realized that the sickle was made for right-handed lavender cutters, and had to compensate for being left-handed by slicing away from me. My wife came out to tell me to mind my legs. She doesn't trust me with sharp implements, and so she was reassured to see me cutting away from the body. Even with my genius for self-inflicted wounds there seemed to be little risk of amputation.

I had just come to the final clump when Henriette came back. I looked up, hoping for praise, and sliced my index finger nearly through to the bone. There was a great deal of blood, and Henriette asked me if I was giving myself a manicure. I sometimes wonder about her sense of humour. Two days later, she gave me a sickle of my very own, and told me that I was forbidden to use it unless I was wearing gloves.

The alcoholic tendencies of wasps

The Provençal wasp, although small, has an evil sting. He also has an ungallant, hit-and-run method of attack in the swimming pool. He paddles up behind his unsuspecting victim, waits until an arm is raised and – *tok!* – strikes deep into the armpit. It hurts for several hours, and often causes people who have been stung to dress in protective clothing before they go swimming. This is the local version of the Miss Wet T-shirt contest.

I don't know whether all wasps like water, but here they love it – floating in the shallow end, dozing in the puddles on the flagstones, keeping an eye out for the unguarded armpit and the tender extremity – and after one disastrous day during which not only armpits but inner thighs received direct hits (obviously, some wasps can hold their breath and operate under water), I was sent off to look for wasp traps.

When I found them, in a *droguerie* in the back alleys of Cavaillon, I was lucky enough to find a wasp expert behind the counter. He demonstrated for me the latest model in traps, a plastic descendant of the old glass hanging traps that can sometimes be found in flea markets. It had been specially designed, he said, for use around swimming pools, and could be made irresistible to wasps.

It was in two parts. The base was a round bowl, raised off the ground by three flat supports, with a funnel leading up from the bottom. The top fitted over the lower bowl and prevented wasps who had made their way up the funnel from escaping.

But that, said the wasp expert, was the simple part. More difficult, more subtle, more artistic, was the bait. How does one persuade the wasp to abandon the pleasures of the flesh and climb up the funnel into the trap? What could tempt him away from the pool?

After spending some time in Provence, you learn to expect a brief lecture with every purchase, from an organically grown cabbage (two minutes) to a bed (half an hour or more, depending on the state of your back). For wasp traps, you should allow between ten and fifteen minutes. I sat back on the stool in front of the counter and listened.

Wasps, it turned out, like alcohol. Some wasps like it *sucré*, others like it fruity, and there are even those who will crawl anywhere for a drop of *anis*. It is, said the expert, a matter of experimentation, a balancing of flavours and consistencies until one finds the blend that suits the palate of the local wasp population.

He suggested a few basic recipes: sweet vermouth with honey and water, diluted *crème de cassis*, dark beer spiked with *marc*, neat *pastis*. As an added inducement, the funnel can be lightly coated with honey, and a small puddle of water should always be left immediately beneath the funnel.

The expert set up a trap on the counter, and with two fingers imitated a wasp out for a stroll.

He stops, attracted by the puddle of water. The fingers stopped. He approaches the water, and then he becomes aware of something delicious above him. He climbs up the funnel to investigate, he jumps into his cocktail, *et voilà!* – he is unable to get out, being too drunk to crawl back down the funnel. He dies, but he dies happy.

I bought two traps, and tried out the recipes. All of them worked, which leads me to believe that the wasp has a serious drinking problem. And now, if ever a guest is overcome by strong waters, he is described as being as pissed as a wasp.

Maladie du Lubéron

Most of the seasonal ailments of summer, while they may be uncomfortable or painful or merely embarrassing, are at least regarded with some sympathy. A man convalescing after an explosive encounter with one *merguez* sausage too many is not expected to venture back into polite society until his constitution has recovered. The same is true of third-degree sunburn, *rosé* poisoning, scorpion bites, a surfeit of garlic or the giddiness and nausea caused by prolonged exposure to French bureaucracy. One suffers, but one is allowed to suffer alone and in peace.

There is another affliction, worse than scorpions or rogue sausages, which we have experienced ourselves and seen many times in other permanent residents of this quiet corner of France. Symptoms usually appear some time around mid-July and persist until early September: glazed and bloodshot eyes, yawning, loss of appetite, shortness of temper, lethargy and a mild form of paranoia which manifests itself in sudden urges to join a monastery.

This is the *maladie du Lubéron*, or creeping social fatigue, and it provokes about the same degree of sympathy as a millionaire's servant problems.

If we examine the patients – the permanent residents – we can see why it happens. Permanent residents have their work, their local friends, their unhurried routines. They made a deliberate choice to live in the Lubéron instead of one of the cocktail capitals of the world because they wanted, if not to get away from it all, to get away from most of it. This eccentricity is understood and tolerated for ten months a year.

Try to explain that in July and August. Here come the visitors, fresh from the plane or hot off the *autoroute*, panting for social action. Let's meet some of the locals! To hell with the book in the hammock and the walk in the woods. To hell with solitude; they want people – people for lunch, people for drinks, people for dinner – and so invitations and counter-invitations fly back and forth until every day for weeks has its own social highlight.

As the holiday comes to an end with one final multi-bottle dinner, it is possible to see even on the visitors' faces some traces of weariness. They had no idea it was so lively down here. They are only half-joking when they say they're going to need a rest to get over the whirl of the past few days. Is it always like this? How do you keep it up?

It isn't, and we don't. Like many of our friends, we collapse in between visitations, guarding empty days and free evenings, eating little and drinking less, going to bed early. And every year, when the dust has settled, we talk to other members of the distressed residents' association about ways of making summer less of an endurance test.

We all agree that firmness is the answer. Say no more often than yes. Harden the heart against the surprise visitor who cannot find an hotel room, the deprived child who has no swimming pool, the desperate traveller who has lost his wallet. Be firm; be helpful, be kind, be rude, but above all *be firm*.

And yet I know – I think we all know – that next summer will be the same. I suppose we must enjoy it. Or we would, if we weren't exhausted.

Place du village

Cars have been banned from the village square, and stalls or trestle tables have been set up on three sides. On the fourth,

a framework of scaffolding, blinking with coloured lights, supports a raised platform made from wooden planks. Outside the café, the usual single row of tables and chairs has been multiplied by ten, and an extra waiter has been taken on to serve the sprawl of customers stretching from the butcher's down to the post office. Children and dogs chase each other through the crowd, stealing lumps of sugar from the tables and dodging the old men's sticks that are waved in mock anger. Nobody will go to bed early tonight, not even the children, because this is the village's annual party, the *fête votive*.

It begins in the late afternoon with a *pot d'amitié* in the square and the official opening of the stalls. Local artisans, the men's faces shining from an afternoon shave, stand behind their tables, glass in hand, or make final adjustments to their displays. There is pottery and jewellery, honey and lavender essence, hand-woven fabrics, iron and stone arte-facts, paintings and wood carvings, books, postcards, tooled leatherwork, corkscrews with twisted olive-wood handles, patterned sachets of dried herbs. The woman selling pizza does brisk business as the first glass of wine begins to make the crowd hungry.

People drift off, eat, drift back. The night comes down, warm and still, the mountains in the distance just visible as deep black humps against the sky. The three-man accordion band tunes up on the platform and launches into the first of many *paso dobles* while the rock group from Avignon that will follow later rehearses on beer and *pastis* in the café.

The first dancers appear -- an old man and his granddaughter, her nose pressed into his belt buckle, her feet balanced precariously on his feet. They are joined by a mother, father and daughter dancing *à trois*, and then by several elderly couples, holding each other with stiff formality, their faces set with concentration as they try to retrace the steps they learned fifty years ago.

The *paso doble* session comes to an end with a flourish and a ruffle of accordion and drums, and the rock group warms up with five minutes of electronic tweaks that bounce off the old stone walls of the church opposite the platform.

The group's singer, a well-built young lady in tight black lycra and a screaming orange wig, has attracted an audience before singing a note. An old man, the peak of his cap almost meeting the jut of his chin, has dragged a chair across from the café to sit directly in front of the microphone. As the singer starts her first number, some village boys made bold by his example come out of the shadows to stand by the old man's chair. All of them stare as though hypnotized at the shiny black pelvis rotating just above their heads.

The village girls, short of partners, dance with each other, as close as possible to the backs of the mesmerized boys. One of the waiters puts down his tray to caper in front of a pretty girl sitting with her parents. She blushes and ducks her head, but her mother nudges her to dance. Go on. The holiday will soon be over.

After an hour of music that threatens to dislodge the windows of the houses round the square, the group performs its finale. With an intensity worthy of Piaf on a sad night, the singer gives us *Comme d'habitude*, or My Way, ending with a sob, her orange head bent over the microphone. The old man nods and bangs his stick on the ground, and the dancers go back to the café to see if there's any beer left.

Normally, there would have been *feux d'artifice* shooting up from the field behind the war memorial. This year, because of the drought, fireworks are forbidden. But it was a good *fête*. And did you see how the postman danced?

18

Arrest That Dog!

A friend in London who occasionally keeps me informed about subjects of international importance which might not be reported in *Le Provençal* sent me a disturbing newspaper clipping. It was taken from *The Times*, and it revealed an enterprise of unspeakable villainy, a knife thrust deep into the most sensitive part of a Frenchman's anatomy.

A gang of scoundrels had been importing white truffles (sometimes contemptuously referred to as 'industrial' truffles) from Italy, and staining them with walnut dye until their complexions were dark enough to pass as black truffles. These, as every gourmet knows, have infinitely more flavour than their white cousins, and cost infinitely more money. *The Times* reporter, I think, had seriously underestimated the prices. He had quoted 400 francs a kilo, which would have caused a stampede at Fauchon in Paris, where I had seen them arranged in the window like jewels at 7,000 francs a kilo.

But that wasn't the point. It was the nature of the crime that mattered. Here were the French, self-appointed world champions of gastronomy, being taken in by counterfeit delicacies, their taste-buds hoodwinked and their wallets plucked clean. Worse still, the fraud didn't even depend on second-class domestic truffles, but on pallid cast-offs from Italy – *Italy*, for God's sake!

I had once heard a Frenchman express his opinion of Italian food in a single libellous phrase: after the noodle, there is nothing. And yet hundreds, maybe thousands, of dusky Italian impersonators had found their way into knowledgeable French stomachs under the crudest of false pretences. The shame of it was enough to make a man weep all over his *foie gras*.

The story reminded me of Alain, who had offered to take me for a day of truffle hunting below Mont Ventoux, and to demonstrate the skills of his miniature pig. But when I called him, he told me he was having a very thin season, the result of the summer drought. *En plus*, the experiment with the pig had been a failure. She was not suited to the work. Nevertheless, he had a few truffles if we were interested, small but good. We arranged to meet in Apt, where he had to see a man about a dog.

There is one café in Apt which is filled, on market day, with men who have truffles to sell. While they wait for customers, they pass the time cheating at cards and lying about how much they were able to charge a passing Parisian for 150 grammes of mud and fungus. They carry folding scales in their pockets, and ancient wooden-handled Opinel knives that are used to cut tiny nicks in the surface of a truffle to prove that its blackness is more than skin-deep. Mixed in with the café smell of coffee and black tobacco is the earthy, almost putrid scent that comes from the contents of the shabby linen bags on the tables. Early morning glasses of *rosé* are sipped, and conversations are often conducted in secretive mutters.

While I waited for Alain, I watched two men crouched over their drinks, their heads close together, glancing around between sentences. One of them took out a cracked Bic pen and wrote something on the palm of his hand. He showed what he had written to the other man and then spat into his palm and carefully rubbed out the evidence. What could it have been? The new price per kilo? The combination of the vault in the bank next door? Or a warning? *Say nothing. A man with glasses is staring at us.*

Alain arrived, and everyone in the café looked at him, as they had looked at me. I felt as though I was about to do something dangerous and illegal instead of buying ingredients for an omelette.

I had brought with me the clipping from *The Times*, but it was old news to Alain. He had heard about it from a friend in the Périgord, where it was causing a great deal of righteous indignation among honest truffle dealers, and grave suspicions in the minds of their customers.

Alain had come to Apt to begin negotiations on the purchase of a new truffle dog. He knew the owner, but not well, and therefore the business would take some time. The asking price was substantial, 20,000 francs, and nothing could be taken on trust. Tests in the field would have to be arranged. The dog's age would have to be established, and his stamina and scenting skills demonstrated. One never knew.

I asked about the miniature pig. Alain shrugged, and drew his index finger across his throat. In the end, he said, unless one was prepared to accept the inconvenience of a full-sized pig, a dog was the only solution. But to find the right dog, a dog that would be worth its weight in banknotes, that was not at all straightforward.

There is no such breed as a truffle hound. Most of the truffle dogs that I had seen were small, nondescript, yappy creatures which looked as though a terrier might have been briefly involved in the bloodline many generations ago. Alain himself had an old Alsatian which, in its day, had worked well. It was all a question of individual instinct and training, and there were no guarantees that a dog who performed for one owner would perform for another. Alain remembered something, and smiled. There was a famous story. I refilled his glass, and he told me.

A man from St Didier once had a dog who could find truffles, so he said, where no other dog had found them before. Throughout the winter, when other hunters were coming back from the hills with a handful, or a dozen, the man from St Didier would return to the café with his satchel bulging. The dog was a *merveille*, and the owner never stopped boasting about his little Napoleon, so called because his nose was worth gold.

Many men coveted Napoleon, but each time they offered to buy him, the owner refused. Until one day, a man came into the café and put four *briques* on the table, four thick wads pinned together, 40,000 francs. This was an extraordinary price and, with a show of reluctance, it was finally accepted. Napoleon went off with his new master.

For the remainder of the season, he didn't find a single truffle. The new owner was *en colère*. He brought Napoleon to the café and demanded his money back. The old owner told him to go away and learn how to hunt properly. Such an *imbécile* didn't deserve a dog like Napoleon. Other unpleasant words were exchanged, but there was no question of the money being refunded.

The new owner went into Avignon to find a lawyer. The

lawyer said, as lawyers often do, that it was a grey area. There was no precedent to refer to, no case in the long and meticulously documented history of French law that touched on the matter of a dog being derelict in his duty. It was without doubt a dispute that would have to be decided by a learned judge.

Months and many consultations later, the two men were instructed to appear in court. The judge, being a thorough and conscientious man, wanted to be sure that all the principals in the case were present. A gendarme was sent to arrest the dog and bring him to court as a material witness.

Whether or not the dog's presence in the witness box helped the judge in his deliberations is not known, but he handed down the following verdict: Napoleon was to be returned to his old owner, who would repay half the purchase price, being allowed to keep the other half as compensation for loss of the dog's services.

Now reunited, Napoleon and his old owner moved from St Didier to a village north of Carpentras. Two years later, an identical case was reported, although due to inflation the amount of money had increased. Napoleon and his owner had done it again.

But there was something I didn't understand. If the dog was such a virtuoso truffle hunter, surely his owner would make more money by working him than selling him, even though he ended up keeping the dog and half the money each time he went to court.

Ah, said Alain, you have assumed, like everyone else, that the truffles in the satchel were found by Napoleon on the days they were brought into the café.

Non?

Non. They were kept in the *congélateur* and brought out

once or twice a week. That dog couldn't find a pork chop in a *charcuterie*. He had a nose of wood.

Alain finished his wine. 'You must never buy a dog in a café. Only when you have seen him work.' He looked at his watch. 'I have time for another glass. And you?'

Always, I said. Did he have another story?

'This you will like, being a writer,' he said. 'It happened many years ago, but I am told it is true.'

The peasant owned a patch of land some distance from his house. It was not a big patch, less than two *hectares*, but it was crowded with ancient oaks, and each winter there were many truffles, enough to allow the peasant to live in comfortable idleness for the rest of the year. His pig barely needed to search. Year after year, truffles grew more or less where they had grown before. It was like finding money under the trees. God was good, and a prosperous old age was assured.

One can imagine the peasant's irritation the first morning he noticed freshly displaced earth under the trees. Something had been on his land during the night, possibly a dog or even a stray pig. A little further on, he noticed a cigarette end crushed into the earth; a modern, filter-tipped cigarette, not of the kind he smoked. And certainly not dropped by a stray pig. This was extremely alarming.

As he went from tree to tree, so his alarm increased. More earth had been disturbed, and he saw fresh grazes on some rocks that could only have been made by a truffle pick.

It wasn't, it couldn't have been, one of his neighbours. He had known them all since childhood. It must have been a foreigner, someone who didn't know that this precious patch was his.

Since he was a reasonable man, he had to admit that there was no way a foreigner could tell if the land was privately owned or not. Fences and signs were expensive, and he had never seen the need for them. His land was his land; everyone knew that. Clearly, times had changed and strangers were finding their way into the hills. He drove to the nearest town that afternoon and bought an armful of signs: *Propriété privée, Défense d'entrer* and, for good measure, three or four that read *Chien méchant*. He and his wife worked until dark nailing them up around the perimeter of the land.

A few days went by without any further signs of the trespasser with the truffle pick, and the peasant allowed himself to relax. It had been an innocent mistake, although he did wonder why an innocent man would hunt truffles at night.

And then it happened again. The signs had been ignored, the land violated and who knows how many fat black nuggets taken from the earth under cover of darkness. It could no longer be excused as the mistake of an ignorant enthusiast. This was a *braconnier*, a poacher, a thief in the night who hoped to profit from an old man's only source of income.

The peasant and his wife discussed the problem that night as they sat in the kitchen and ate their *soupe*. They could, of course, call in the police. But since truffles – or at least, the money made from selling the truffles – did not officially exist, it might not be prudent to involve the authorities. Questions would be asked about the value of what had been stolen, and private information such as this was best kept private. Besides, the official penalty for truffle poaching, even if it were a spell in jail, would not replace the thousands of francs that were even now stuffed in the poacher's deep and dishonest pockets.

And so the couple decided to seek tougher but more

satisfactory justice, and the peasant went to see two of his neighbours, men who would understand what needed to be done.

They agreed to help him, and for several long, cold nights the three of them waited with their shotguns among the truffle oaks, coming home each dawn slightly tipsy from the *marc* that they had been obliged to drink to keep out the chill. At last, one night when clouds scudded across the face of the moon and the Mistral bit into the faces of the three men, they saw the headlights of a car. It stopped at the end of a dirt track, 200 metres down the hill.

The engine stopped, lights were extinguished, doors opened and quietly closed. There were voices, and then the glow of a torch, which came slowly up the hill towards them.

First into the trees was a dog. He stopped, picked up the scent of the men and barked – a high, nervous bark, followed at once by *ssssst!* as the poacher hissed him quiet. The men flexed their numb fingers for a better grip of their guns, and the peasant took aim with the torch he had brought specially for the ambush.

The beam caught them as they came into the clearing: a couple, middle-aged and unremarkable, the woman carrying a small sack, the man with torch and truffle pick. Red-handed.

The three men, making great display of their artillery, approached the couple. They had no defence, and with gun barrels under their noses quickly admitted that they had been before to steal truffles.

How many truffles? asked the old peasant. Two kilos? Five kilos? More?

Silence from the poachers, and silence from the three men as they thought about what they should do. Justice must be done; more important than justice, money must be repaid. One of the men whispered in the old peasant's ear, and he nodded. Yes, that is what we will do. He announced the verdict of the impromptu court.

Where was the poacher's bank? Nyons? *Ah bon*. If you start walking now you will be there when it opens. You will take out 30,000 francs, which you will bring back here. We shall keep your car and your dog and your wife until you return.

The poacher set off on the four-hour walk to Nyons. His dog was put in the boot of the car, his wife in the back seat. The three men squeezed in too. It was a cold night. They dozed through it in between tots of *marc*.

Dawn came, then morning, then noon . . .

Alain stopped his story. 'You're a writer,' he said. 'How do you think it ended?'

I made a couple of guesses, both wrong, and Alain laughed.

'It was very simple, not at all *dramatique*,' he said. 'Except perhaps for the wife. The poacher went to his bank in Nyons and took out all the money he possessed, and then – *pouf!* – he disappeared.'

'He never came back?'

'Nobody ever saw him again.'

'Not his wife?'

'Certainly not his wife. He was not fond of his wife.'

'And the peasant?'

'He died an angry man.'

Alain said he had to go. I paid him for the truffles, and wished him luck with his new dog. When I got home, I cut one of the truffles in half to make sure it was the genuine, deep black all the way through. He seemed like a good fellow, Alain, but you never know.

19

Life Through Rosé-tinted Spectacles

Going native.

I don't know whether it was meant as a joke, an insult or a compliment, but that was what the man from London said. He had dropped in unexpectedly on his way to the coast, and stayed for lunch. We hadn't seen him for five years, and he was obviously curious to see what effects life in Provence was having on us, examining us thoughtfully for signs of moral and physical deterioration.

We weren't conscious of having changed, but he was sure of it, although there was nothing he could put his finger on. For lack of any single change as plain as delirium tremens, rusty English or premature senility, he put us in the vague, convenient and all-embracing pigeonhole marked 'going native'.

As he drove away in his clean car, telephone antenna fluttering gaily in the breeze, I looked at our small and dusty Citroën, which was innocent of any communications facility. That was certainly a native car. And, in comparison with our visitor's Côte d'Azur outfit, I was wearing native dress – old shirt, shorts, no shoes. Then I remembered how often he had looked at his watch during lunch, because he was meeting friends at Nice at 6.30. Not later in the day, not some time that evening, but at 6.30. Precisely. We had long ago abandoned time-keeping of such a high standard due to lack of local support, and now lived according to the rules of the approximate rendezvous. Another native habit.

The more I thought about it, the more I realized that we must have changed. I wouldn't have called it going native, but there are dozens of differences between our old life and our new life, and we have had to adjust to them. It hasn't been difficult. Most of the changes have taken place gradually, pleasantly, almost imperceptibly. All of them, I think, are changes for the better.

We no longer watch television. It wasn't a self-righteous decision to give us time for more intellectual pursuits; it simply happened. In the summer, watching television can't begin to compare with watching the evening sky. In the winter, it can't compete with dinner. The television set has now been relegated to a cupboard to make space for more books.

We eat better than we used to, and probably more cheaply. It is impossible to live in France for any length of time and stay immune to the national enthusiasm for food, and who would want to? Why not make a daily pleasure out of a daily necessity? We have slipped into the gastronomic rhythm of Provence, taking advantage of the special offers provided by nature all through the year: asparagus, tiny *haricots verts* barely thicker than matchsticks, fat *fèves*, cherries, aubergines, *courgettes*, peppers, peaches and apricots and melons and grapes, *blette*, wild mushrooms, olives, truffles – every season brings its own treat. With the expensive exception of the truffle, nothing costs more than a few francs a kilo.

Meat is a different matter, and butchers' prices can make

the visitor wince. Provence is not cattle country, and so the Englishman in search of his roast beef on Sunday had better take his cheque book and be prepared for disappointment, because the beef is neither cheap nor tender. But lamb, above all from the area round Sisteron where the sheep season themselves with herbs, has a taste that it would be a crime to disguise with mint sauce. And every part of the pig is good.

Even so, we now eat less meat. An occasional *appellation contrôlée* chicken from Bresse, the wild rabbits that Henriette brings in the winter, a *cassoulet* when the temperature drops and the Mistral howls round the house – meat from time to time is wonderful. Meat every day is a habit of the past. There is so much else: fish from the Mediterranean, fresh pasta, limitless recipes for all those vegetables, dozens of breads, hundreds of cheeses.

It may be the change in our diet and the way it is cooked, always in olive oil, but we have both lost weight. Only a little, but enough to cause some surprise to friends who expect us to have developed the ballooning *embonpoint* – the stomach on stilts – that sometimes grows on people with good appetites who have the luck to eat in France.

Through no deliberate intention of our own, we also take more exercise. Not the grim contortions promoted by gaunt women in leotards, but the exercise which comes naturally from living in a climate that allows you to spend eight or nine months of the year outdoors. Discipline has nothing to do with it, apart from the small disciplines of country life – bringing logs in for the fire, keeping the weeds down and the ditches clear, planting, pruning, bending and lifting. And, every day in every kind of weather, walking.

We have had people to stay who refuse to believe that

walking can be hard exercise. It's not dramatic effort, not immediately punishing, not fast, not violent. Everybody walks, they say. You can't call that exercise. Eventually, if they insist, we take them out for a stroll with the dogs.

For the first ten minutes the going is flat, along the footpath at the bottom of the mountain, easy and undemanding. Pleasant to get a little fresh air and a view of Mont Ventoux in the distance. But exercise? They're not even short of breath.

Then we turn and go up the track leading to the cedar forest that grows along the spine of the Lubéron. The surface changes from sandy soil cushioned with pine needles to rocks and patches of scree, and we begin to climb. After five minutes, there are no more condescending remarks about walking being an old man's exercise. After ten minutes, there are no remarks at all, only the sound of increasingly heavy breathing, punctuated by coughing. The track twists around boulders and under branches so low you have to bend double. There is no encouraging glimpse of the top; the view is limited to a hundred yards or so of narrow, stony, steeply inclined track before it disappears round the next outcrop of rock. If there is any breath to spare, there might be a curse as an ankle turns on the shifting scree. Legs and lungs are burning.

The dogs pad on ahead, with the rest of us strung out behind them at irregular intervals, the least fit stumbling along with their backs bent and their hands on their thighs. Pride usually prevents them from stopping, and they wheeze away stubbornly, heads down, feeling sick. They will never again dismiss walking as non-exercise.

The prize when you reach the top is to find yourself in a silent, extraordinary landscape, sometimes eerie, always

beautiful. The cedars are magnificent, and magical when they are draped with great swags of snow. Beyond them, on the south face of the mountain, the land drops away sharply, grey and jagged, softened by the thyme and box that seem to be able to grow in the most unpromising wrinkle of rock.

On a clear day, when the Mistral has blown and the air shines, the views towards the sea are long and sharply focused, almost as if they have been magnified, and there is a sense of being hundreds of miles away from the rest of the world. I once met a peasant up there, on the road the forest service made through the cedars. He was on an old bicycle, a gun slung across his back, a dog loping beside him. We were both startled to see another human being. It is normally less busy, and the only sound is the wind nagging at the trees.

The days pass slowly but the weeks rush by. We now measure the year in ways that have little to do with diaries and specific dates. There is the almond blossom in February, and a few weeks of pre-spring panic in the garden as we try to do the work we've been talking about doing all winter. Spring is a mixture of cherry blossom and a thousand weeds and the first guests of the year, hoping for sub-tropical weather and often getting nothing but rain and wind. Summer might start in April. It might start in May. We know it's arrived when Bernard calls to help us uncover and clean the pool.

Poppies in June, drought in July, storms in August. The vines begin to turn rusty, the hunters come out of their summer hibernation, the grapes have been picked and the water in the pool nips more and more fiercely until it becomes too cold for anything more than a masochistic plunge in the middle of the day. It must be the end of October.

Winter is filled with good resolutions, and some of them are actually achieved. A dead tree is cut down, a wall is built, the old steel garden chairs are repainted, and whenever there is time to spare we take up the dictionary and resume our struggle with the French language.

Our French has improved, and the thought of spending an evening in totally French company is not as daunting as it used to be. But, to use the words that were so often used in my school reports, there is considerable room for improvement. Must try harder. And so we inch our way through books by Pagnol and Giono and de Maupassant, buy *Le Provençal* regularly, listen to the machine-gun delivery of radio news-readers and attempt to unravel the mysteries of what we are constantly being told is a supremely logical language.

I think that is a myth, invented by the French to bewilder foreigners. Where is the logic, for instance, in the genders given to proper names and nouns? Why is the Rhône masculine and the Durance feminine? They are both rivers, and if they must have a sex, why can't it be the same one? When I asked a Frenchman to explain this to me, he delivered a dissertation on sources, streams and floods which, according to him, answered the question conclusively and, of course, logically. Then he went on to the masculine ocean, the feminine sea, the masculine lake and the feminine puddle. Even the water must get confused.

His speech did nothing to change my theory, which is that genders are there for no other reason than to make life difficult. They have been allocated in a whimsical and arbitrary fashion, sometimes with a cavalier disregard for the anatomical niceties. The French for vagina is *vagin*. *Le vagin*. Masculine. How can the puzzled student hope to apply logic to a language in which the vagina is masculine?

There is also the androgynous *lui* waiting to ambush us at the threshold of many a sentence. Normally, *lui* is him. In some constructions, *lui* is her. Often, we are left in the dark as to *lui*'s gender until it is made known to us some time after he or she has been introduced, as in: '*Je lui ai téléphoné* (I called him), '*mais elle était occupée*' (but she was busy). A short-lived mystery, possibly, but one which can trip up the novice, particularly when *lui*'s first name is also a mixture of masculine and feminine, such as Jean-Marie or Marie-Pierre.

And that is not the worst of it. Strange and unnatural events take place every day within the formalities of French syntax. A recent newspaper article, reporting on the marriage of the rock singer Johnny Hallyday, paused in its description of the bride's frock to give Johnny a pat on the back. '*Il est,*' said the article, '*une grande vedette.*' In the space of a single short sentence, the star had undergone a sex change, and on his wedding day too.

It is perhaps because of these perplexing twists and turns that French was for centuries the language of diplomacy, an occupation in which simplicity and clarity are not regarded as being necessary, or even desirable. Indeed, the guarded statement, made fuzzy by formality and open to several different interpretations, is much less likely to land an ambassador in the soup than plain words which mean what they say. A diplomat, according to Alex Dreier, is 'anyone who thinks twice before saying nothing'. Nuance and significant vagueness are essential, and French might have been invented to allow these linguistic weeds to flourish in the crevices of every sentence.

But it is a beautiful, supple and romantic language, although it may not quite deserve the reverence that inspires a course of French lessons to be described as a '*cours de civilisation*' by those who regard it as a national treasure and a shining example of how everyone should speak. One can imagine the dismay of these purists at the foreign horrors that are now creeping into everyday French.

The rot probably started when *le weekend* slipped across the Channel to Paris at about the same time that a night-club owner in Pigalle christened his establishment *Le Sexy*. Inevitably, this led to the naughty institution of *le weekend sexy*, to the delight of Parisian hotel owners and the despair of their counterparts in Brighton and other less erotically blessed resorts.

The invasion of the language hasn't stopped in the bed-room. It has also infiltrated the office. The executive now has *un job*. If the pressure of work becomes too much for him, he will find himself increasingly *stressé*, perhaps because of the demands of being *un leader* in the business jungle of *le marketing*. The poor, overworked wretch doesn't even have time for the traditional three-hour lunch, and has to make do with *le fast-food*. It is the worst kind of Franglais, and it goads the elders of the Académie Française into fits of outrage. I can't say I blame them. These clumsy intrusions into such a graceful language are *scandaleux*; or, to put it another way, *les pits*.

The gradual spread of Franglais is helped by the fact that there are many fewer words in the French vocabulary than in English. This has its own set of problems, because the same word can have more than one meaning. In Paris, for instance, '*je suis ravi*' will normally be taken to mean 'I am delighted.' In the Café du Progrès in Ménerbes, however, *ravi* has a second, uncomplimentary translation, and the same phrase can mean 'I am the village idiot.'

In order to disguise my confusion and to avoid at least some of the many verbal booby-traps, I have learned to grunt like a native, to make those short but expressive sounds – those sharp intakes of breath, those understanding clickings of the tongue, those mutters of *beh oui* –that are used like conversational stepping stones in between one subject and the next.

Of all these, the most flexible and therefore most useful is the short and apparently explicit phrase *ah bon*, used with or without a question mark. I used to think this meant what it said, but of course it doesn't. A typical exchange, with the right degree of catastrophe and gloom, might go something like this:

'Young Jean-Pierre is in real trouble this time.'

'*Oui?*'

'*Beh oui*. He came out of the café, got in his car, ran over a *gendarme* – completely *écrasé* –drove into a wall, went through the windscreen, split his head open and broke his leg in fourteen places.'

'*Ah bon.*'

Depending on inflection, *ah bon* can express shock, disbelief, indifference, irritation or joy – a remarkable achievement for two short words.

Similarly, it is possible to conduct the greater part of a brief conversation with two other monosyllables – *ça va* – which mean literally 'it goes'. Every day, in every town and village around Provence, acquaintances will meet on the street, perform the ritual handshake and deliver the ritual dialogue:

'*Ça va?*'

'*Oui. Ça va, ça va. Et vous?*'

'*Bohf, ça va.*'

'*Bieng. Ça va alors.*'
'*Oui, oui. Ça va.*'
'*Allez. Au 'voir.*'
'*Au 'voir.*'

The words alone do not do justice to the occasion, which is decorated with shrugs and sighs and thoughtful pauses that can stretch to two or three minutes if the sun is shining and there is nothing pressing to do. And, naturally, the same unhurried, pleasant acknowledgement of neighbourhood faces will be repeated several times in the course of the morning's errands.

It is easy to be misled, after a few months of these uncomplicated encounters, into believing that you are beginning to distinguish yourself in colloquial French. You may even have spent long evenings with French people who profess to understand you. They become more than acquaintances; they become friends. And when they judge the moment is ripe, they present you with the gift of friendship in spoken form, which brings with it an entirely new set of opportunities to make a fool of yourself. Instead of using *vous*, they will start addressing you as *tu* or *toi*, a form of intimacy that has its own verb, *tutoyer*.

The day when a Frenchman switches from the formality of *vous* to the familiarity of *tu* is a day to be taken seriously. It is an unmistakable signal that he has decided – after weeks or months or sometimes years – that he likes you. It would be churlish and unfriendly of you not to return the compliment. And so, just when you are at last feeling reasonably comfortable with *vous* and all the plurals that go with it, you are thrust headlong into the singular world of *tu*. (Unless, of course, you follow the example of ex-President Giscard d'Estaing, who apparently addresses even his wife as *vous*.)

But we stumble along, committing all kinds of sins against grammar and gender, making long and awkward detours to avoid the swamps of the subjunctive and the chasms in our vocabularies, hoping that our friends are not too appalled at the mauling we give their language. They are kind enough to say that our French doesn't make them shudder. I doubt that, but there is no doubting their desire to help us feel at home, and there is a warmth to everyday life that is not just the sun.

That, at least, has been our experience. It obviously isn't universal, and some people either don't believe it, or even seem to resent it. We have been accused of the crime of cheerfulness, of turning a blind eye to minor problems, and of deliberately ignoring what is invariably described as the dark side of the Provençal character. This ominous cliché is wheeled out and festooned with words like dishonest, lazy, bigoted, greedy and brutal. It is as if they are peculiarly local characteristics which the innocent foreigner – honest, industrious, unprejudiced and generally blameless – will be exposed to for the first time in his life.

It is of course true that there are crooks and bigots in Provence, just as there are crooks and bigots everywhere. But we've been lucky, and Provence has been good to us. We will never be more than permanent visitors in someone else's country, but we have been made welcome and happy. There are no regrets, few complaints, many pleasures.

Merci Provence.

All Pan Books are available at your local bookshop or newsagent, or can be ordered direct from the publisher. Indicate the number of copies required and fill in the form below.

Send to: Pan C. S. Dept
                Macmillan Distribution Ltd
                Houndmills Basingstoke RG21 2XS
or phone: 0256 29242, quoting title, author and Credit Card number.

Please enclose a remittance* to the value of the cover price plus £1.00 for the first book plus 50p per copy for each additional book ordered.

* Payment may be made in sterling by UK personal cheque, postal order, sterling draft or international money order, made payable to Pan Books Ltd.

Alternatively by Barclaycard/Access/Amex/Diners

Card No. ☐☐☐☐☐☐☐☐☐☐☐☐☐☐☐☐☐☐☐

Expiry Date ☐☐☐☐☐☐

_____

Signature

Applicable only in the UK and BFPO addresses.

While every effort is made to keep prices low, it is sometimes necessary to increase prices at short notice. Pan Books reserve the right to show on covers and charge new retail prices which may differ from those advertised in the text or elsewhere.

NAME AND ADDRESS IN BLOCK LETTERS PLEASE

....

Name _____

Address_____

_____

_____

_____

3/87